Palgrave Studies in International Relations

Series Editors
Mai'a K. Davis Cross, Northeastern University, Boston, MA, USA
Benjamin de Carvalho, Norwegian Institute of International Affairs,
Oslo, Norway
Shahar Hameiri, University of Queensland, St. Lucia, QLD, Australia
Knud Erik Jørgensen, University of Aarhus, Aarhus, Denmark
Ole Jacob Sending, Norwegian Institute of International Affairs,
Oslo, Norway
Ayşe Zarakol, University of Cambridge, Cambridge, UK

Palgrave Studies in International Relations (the EISA book series), published in association with European International Studies Association, provides scholars with the best theoretically-informed scholarship on the global issues of our time. The series includes cutting-edge monographs and edited collections which bridge schools of thought and cross the boundaries of conventional fields of study. EISA members can access a 50% discount to PSIR, the EISA book series, here http://www.eisa-net.org/sitecore/content/be-bruga/mci-registrations/eisa/login/landing.aspx.

Mai'a K. Davis Cross is the Edward W. Brooke Professor of Political Science at Northeastern University, USA, and Senior Researcher at the ARENA Centre for European Studies, University of Oslo, Norway.

Benjamin de Carvalho is a Senior Research Fellow at the Norwegian Institute of International Affairs (NUPI), Norway.

Shahar Hameiri is Associate Professor of International Politics and Associate Director of the Graduate Centre in Governance and International Affairs, School of Political Science and International Studies, University of Queensland, Australia.

Knud Erik Jørgensen is Professor of International Relations at Aarhus University, Denmark, and at Yaşar University, Izmir, Turkey.

Ole Jacob Sending is the Research Director at the Norwegian Institute of International Affairs (NUPI), Norway.

Ayşe Zarakol is Reader in International Relations at the University of Cambridge and a fellow at Emmanuel College, UK.

More information about this series at
http://www.palgrave.com/gp/series/14619

William Mallinson

Guicciardini, Geopolitics and Geohistory

Understanding Inter-State Relations

William Mallinson
Athens, Greece

Palgrave Studies in International Relations
ISBN 978-3-030-76536-1   ISBN 978-3-030-76537-8 (eBook)
https://doi.org/10.1007/978-3-030-76537-8

© The Editor(s) (if applicable) and The Author(s), under exclusive license to Springer Nature Switzerland AG 2021
This work is subject to copyright. All rights are solely and exclusively licensed by the Publisher, whether the whole or part of the material is concerned, specifically the rights of translation, reprinting, reuse of illustrations, recitation, broadcasting, reproduction on microfilms or in any other physical way, and transmission or information storage and retrieval, electronic adaptation, computer software, or by similar or dissimilar methodology now known or hereafter developed.
The use of general descriptive names, registered names, trademarks, service marks, etc. in this publication does not imply, even in the absence of a specific statement, that such names are exempt from the relevant protective laws and regulations and therefore free for general use.
The publisher, the authors and the editors are safe to assume that the advice and information in this book are believed to be true and accurate at the date of publication. Neither the publisher nor the authors or the editors give a warranty, expressed or implied, with respect to the material contained herein or for any errors or omissions that may have been made. The publisher remains neutral with regard to jurisdictional claims in published maps and institutional affiliations.

Cover illustration: © Melisa Hasan

This Palgrave Macmillan imprint is published by the registered company Springer Nature Switzerland AG
The registered company address is: Gewerbestrasse 11, 6330 Cham, Switzerland

Foreword

A Historian and His Changing Time

Politics is anything but permanency. Whenever one tries to catch the political spirit of the time by the tail, it shirks away. William Mallinson's new book wonderfully catches this paradox by showing that only history exists. Our willingness to see world politics as a stable and conceivable system of relations is a logical shortcut. Humanity has always tended to stereotype social reality around us by turning complex processes into comprehensible thoughts and explanations.

It is no coincidence that Francesco Guicciardini is the centrepiece of the book, a starting point from which Professor Mallinson draws his diverging circles. Guicciardini lived in one of the grandest laboratories of ideas of his time. Florence was not only a major intellectual capital in Europe, but also an intersection of competing political interests, intrigues and insurgencies. Like his great compatriot Niccolò Machiavelli, Guicciardini was witnessing history in the making. It was a decisive turning point for the future of the Italian city-states that were gradually losing their independence due to external pressures and internal struggles. Guicciardini was not a mere political insider describing the political machinery; he also envisioned the complexity of factors shaping the political moment. His approach to analysing political relations through historical interdependencies and human behaviour has never lost its relevance.

Five centuries on, through the Enlightenment, the emergence of nation-states, and hundreds of wars and revolutions, humanity is still unable to construct a predictable and permanent order. The decline of global liberalism that for some time had been seen as a high point of progress is just another parallel to Guicciardini's era of republican demise. One rule that the Renaissance thinker teaches is that republics are strong as long as they preserve internal unity. The more offensively fractious societies become, the more vulnerable they are, as well as the order upon which they rest.

Professor Mallinson does not intend to portray the global zeitgeist or concentrate on a particular historical moment, although he does provide us with numerous historical examples. His main goal is to demonstrate the relativity and complexity of world politics as a never-ending and changing process, in accordance with repeating of modified patterns.

Hence his criticism of realism as a theory claiming to have a rational explanation of interstate relations through the lens of static balance of power. Another critical arrow flies towards geopolitics, with its geographical determinism. These two paradigms have not only oversimplified world politics, and bestowed states with obscure features such as state behaviour and the creation of gargantuan concepts like the national interest, but have also led to the construction of a new normative order in which national interests serve as legitimators of hyper-securitisation at home and egoistic actions abroad.

Geohistory, the main approach used in the book, is not a magic solution to solve the complexities of world politics, but offers a fresh look at how to apprehend these complexities. No doubt history is a powerful analytical tool that could and should be used, if not to draw direct parallels with the past and learn from previous mistakes, but rather to gain a sense of how our understanding of norms and principles constituting the framework of international relations changes and adapts (or has been adapted) to certain political moments. Guicciardini saw history as a guidebook that could be read in different ways, but he never offered linear explanations.

Professor Mallinson reintroduces the spirit of Guicciardini's thought to show that *raison d'être* and realistic interests are not enough to predict state actions which are inevitably driven by human behaviour. History, if analysed correctly and not blurred by ideology, has the ability to explain the way humans, groups and states build the present. Mainstream international relations theories are once again stuck in their paradigms, unable to ascertain why the whole system of world politics moves in a direction that nobody could predict even a decade ago. This book is a long-needed critique and thoughtful provocation for further and deeper discussion.

Pavel Kanevskiy
Professor of Political Science, Associate Dean
Faculty of Sociology, Lomonosov Moscow State University,
Moscow, Russia

Acknowledgements I thank Francesco Guicciardini for his circumspection and wisdom, and Zoran Ristic for his encouragement, comments and advice on my text.

'Peace and Conflict', by the artist David Mallinson

Contents

1	**Explanation**	1
	Introduction	2
	Misinterpreting Machiavelli et al.	3
	Conceptual Frameworks	6
	Conclusions	9
	Bibliography	12
2	**Who Is Guicciardini?**	15
	Introduction	15
	Human Characteristics and Behaviour	17
	Guicciardini's History	20
	Fortune	24
	Conclusions	25
	Bibliography	28
3	**The War of the Theories**	31
	Introduction	32
	Realists and Behaviouralists	32
	Mental Mess	35
	Attempt to Clarify	38
	Conclusions	38
	Bibliography	42
4	**Geopolitics and the Politicisation of Geography**	43
	Introduction	43

	Defining Geopolitics	44
	Politicisation of Geography	46
	Supremacy	48
	Surfeit of Logic	49
	Haushofer	50
	The Return of Geopolitics	51
	The World Island Hits Back	53
	Critique	54
	Now Is then	55
	Bibliography	65
5	**Casualties of Geopolitics**	67
	Introduction	67
	Cyprus as a Strategic Cat's Paw	68
	Iraq and Oil	74
	Strategy, Greed and Oil	77
	Conclusions	79
	Bibliography	82
6	**Geohistory**	85
	Introduction	85
	Only History Exists	86
	The Human Connexion	87
	Appearances	91
	Connecting	92
	Conclusions	94
	Bibliography	97
7	**The Effects of Globalisation**	99
	Introduction	100
	Information Explosion	100
	The End of Meaning?	101
	Technology, Speed and Greed	105
	The Attack on Diplomacy	110
	Conclusions	115
	Bibliography	117
8	**The Ricordi and Memory**	119
	Introduction	119
	History and Memory	121
	Documents	123

Atavism and Nostalgia	127
Identity	129
Nationalism	131
National or State Interests?	132
Foreign Policy, Diplomacy and Secrecy	134
Conclusions	136
Bibliography	140
Bibliography	141
Index	147

LIST OF FIGURES

Fig. 3.1	Confusion illustration by the artist David Mallinson	33
Fig. 3.2	The scramble for IR, by the artist David Mallinson	40
Fig. 5.1	Dependence, illustration by the artist David Mallinson	69
Fig. 8.1	Guicciardini through the Ages, by the artist-illustrator Alice Mallinson	137

CHAPTER 1

Explanation

Abstract This chapter provides the reader with a foretaste of what is to come. It introduces the reader to Guicciardini and his *Ricordi*, juxtaposing him with Machiavelli, and explaining how the former will be the main vehicle to help to understand relations between states. It will suggest that geopolitics is inadequate in gaining a deep understanding of inter-state relations. The chapter introduces the term 'geohistory', with its emphasis on the immutability of human nature and characteristics, and advocates the importance of detaching oneself from ideology and 'conceptual frameworks', and of scrutinising documents.

Keywords Guicciardini · Machiavelli · Geohistory · Geopolitics · Inter-state relations

The simple way of considering matters, which is so much the example of a noble nature, was seen as an absurd characteristic, and soon died.[1]
                                                                            Thucydides

© The Author(s), under exclusive license to Springer Nature Switzerland AG 2021
W. Mallinson, *Guicciardini, Geopolitics and Geohistory*, Palgrave Studies in International Relations, https://doi.org/10.1007/978-3-030-76537-8_1

Introduction

This book aims to demonstrate that geohistory, as opposed to geopolitics, is a more effective concept in understanding relations between states, at a time of considerable confusion in world affairs, and that Francesco Guicciardini's thoughts are an efficient medium to demonstrate not only the inadequacies of geopolitics, but that a geohistorical approach can be a more responsible way of understanding international affairs. Most important, the book introduces a fresh approach and concept, namely geohistory, an approach which I posit is based on the individual, on which corporate characteristics and behaviour depend, often in the shape of state interests. Geohistory diverges strongly from the hackneyed and simplistic assumption that relations between states are based exclusively on balance of power and state interests, neither being easy to define with precision, being too broad brush, with the wood ignoring the trees, branches, twigs, buds and flowers.

The book is intended for those wishing to better understand the reality of relations between countries and sets out to escape from conformist, conventional (and even allegedly unconventional) theories of international relations, theories that, for all their usefulness as thought-provokers, appear increasingly to have exacerbated the confusion of the state of the world in recent times. The book will therefore aim to inject common sense into the complicated equation, and negotiate a coherent theory-, model-and ideology-free path towards understanding relations between states: a path consisting of the hard study of history, mainly through documents, in tandem with a recognition that human characteristics and the behaviour resulting from those characteristics, both individual and corporate, provide the most reliable starting point and answer to aiding this understanding, unlike over-reliance on ideology, which can be a way of hiding one's weaknesses, even from oneself, through substitute thinking. Fixation with theories, as well as with a particular ideology, can subliminally imprison the mind in expedient 'conceptual frameworks', thereby detracting from truly free and detached understanding. And those who claim to think 'outside the box' may in fact depend upon that very box, in order to think outside it. This book has no truck with a box. Its mental underpinning is Francesco Guicciardini's *Ricordi* (*Counsels and Reflections*).[2] A precise and more apt translation of 'ricordi' actually gives us 'memories' and therefore the link to geohistory,[3] on which we shall elaborate in a separate chapter. Our guide will be history *pur et simple*, in other words the past, which begins now. What we call 'the present' is our awareness of the past, of history in its purest and most basic meaning. In this sense, only history, the past, exists. The present is simply our awareness of history, and the future becomes history as it occurs. When and if you reach the end of this book, my hope is that you will then read Guicciardini's *Ricordi*, bring his thought back to life, and even bring him the credit that he deserves.

Misinterpreting Machiavelli et al.

Guicciardini is not exactly a household name today, in the same way as his contemporary compatriot Niccolò Machiavelli's name is. One reason for this could be that Machiavelli's *The Prince* was published only five years after his death, while Guicciardini's *Ricordi* was published over three hundred years later. Another reason could be that *The Prince's* exposure of the reality and dark side of human behaviour, and thus its notoriety, has attracted international relations pundits, especially those trying to justify power politics/political realism[4] and geopolitics (a primitive form of International Relations theory).[5] They cherry-pick from Machiavelli's *The Prince*, as they often do from Thomas Hobbes' *Leviathan*. Leo Strauss, for example, writes that Machiavelli 'ostensibly seeks to bring about the rebirth of the ancient Roman Republic'.[6] A detached thinker might consider this to be sophistic chicanery, since Machiavelli's dream was to unite Italy and Italians, not to reconquer the Hellenic world, Gaul et al. As for Hobbes, another key figure for political realists, he was concerned with the internal power structures of England and with justifying his view of absolutism, rather than with conquering foreign lands. Even the historian Thucydides does not escape the attention of supporters of political realism: one book[7] tries to transmogrify him into an international relations theorist on strategy, thereby diverting attention from the fact that he was simply a general who wrote a history of some wars, whose aim, in his own words, was to help 'those who want to understand clearly the events which happened in the past and which (human nature being what it is) will, at some time or other and in much the same ways, be repeated in the future'.[8] As we shall see, this is very much in line with Guicciardini's thinking. The latter is not even mentioned in any of Henry Kissinger's[9] rather verbose books, whereas Machiavelli is, since Kissinger appears to think that *The Prince* is directly relevant to today's world, and that it fits in with his 'geo-thinking'.[10] He would probably also agree with the Athenian delegate at Sparta, recorded by Thucydides as saying that it had always been a rule that the weak should be subject to the strong.[11] But we need to make the point here that Thucydides himself was probably no lover of the use of force per se by the strong against the weak. Rather, his own view was that what made war inevitable was the growth of Athenian power and the fear which this caused in Sparta.[12] Indeed, he bewailed war. Seeking any justification by Thucydides' for the strong attacking the weak, especially unilaterally, is therefore clutching at straws. Rather, his comments on the reasons for war are based on the human aspect, rather than on promoting the idea of the strong attacking the weak. We can see this clearly when he wrote, for example that love of power, operating through greed and through personal ambition, was the cause of all these evils'[13] and that had it 'not been for the pernicious power of envy, men would not so have exalted vengeance above innocence and profit above justice'.[14] As we shall see, Guicciardini's thinking is also more in line with an understanding of human nature, and therefore explaining war, than in justifying it. Let us expand a little more on the similarities and differences between Guicciardini and Machiavelli.

Discussing fortune, they clearly have a different approach. Machiavelli wrote: '[…] it is better to be impetuous than cautious, because fortune is a woman, and it is necessary, in order to keep her down, to beat her and to struggle with her. And it is seen that she more often allows herself to be taken over by men who are impetuous than by those who make cold advances; […]'.[15] In contrast, Guicciardini writes: 'Whoso well considers it will scarce deny that in human affairs Fortune rules supreme. For every hour we find the most momentous results springing from such fortuitous causes as it was not within the power of man either to foresee or to escape. And although discernment and vigilance may temper many things, they cannot do so unhelped, but stand always in need of favourable Fortune'.[16]

On a ruler's image, we see similarities. According to Machiavelli, '[…] A prince […] should appear […] to be all mercy, all faithfulness, all integrity, all kindness, all religion. […] Everyone sees what you seem to be, few touch upon what you are […]'. In a similar vein, Guicciardini writes; 'Let him who is employed in important affairs and looks to make his way in the world, conceal mishaps and magnify successes'.[17] We see here that both men, who were known to be virtuous in their private lives, see state matters as a different kettle altogether, in that deception can be a necessary tool in maintaining a good reputation.[18]

Machiavelli comes across as more ambitious, and even emotional, in his hopes than Guicciardini, who modestly writes that before he dies, he would willingly see a well-ordered republic established in Florence and an Italy freed from all her barbarian invaders.[19] But Machiavelli calls for the liberation of all Italy, also writing: 'For everyone, this barbarian domination stinks!'.[20]

A comment on fear gives us some further insight into the two Florentines. Machiavelli writes that it is much safer to be feared than loved, continuing: 'A prince must nevertheless make himself feared in such a manner that he will avoid hatred, even if he does not acquire love; since to be feared and not to be hated can very well be combined; and this will always be so when he keeps his hands off the property and the women of his citizens and his subjects'.[21] Guicciardini writes: 'It is no marvel that a governor who frequently resorts to cruelty and harshness should make himself feared. For his subjects are likely enough to fear one who has it in his power to use violence against them, or to ruin them, and whom is not slow to smite. Those governors I commend who, while they inflict few severities or punishments, yet know how to acquire and preserve a name for strictness'.[22] What comes across is that while both men acknowledge fear and punishment as an inevitable part of ruling, Guicciardini would prefer a ruler to be respected for being strict, rather than feared for violence.

We can also identify a difference in approach between the two men to sincerity and lying. Machiavelli justifies lying and breaking promises thus: 'A prince never lacks legitimate reasons to break his promise [...] but it is necessary to know how to disguise this nature well and to be a great hypocrite and a liar: and men are so simple-minded and so controlled by their present needs that one who deceives will always find another who will allow himself to be deceived'.[23] Guicciardini is more circumspect: 'Frank sincerity is a quality much extolled among men and pleasing to everyone, while simulation, on the contrary, is detested and condemned. Yet for a man's self, simulation is of the two by far the more useful; sincerity tending rather to the interest of others. But since it cannot be denied that it is not a fine thing to be deceived, I would commend him whose conduct is as a rule open and straightforward, and who used simulation only in matters of the gravest importance and such as very seldom occur; for in this way he will gain a name for honesty and sincerity, and with it the advantages attaching to these qualities. At the same time, when, in any extreme emergency, he resorts to simulation, he will draw all the greater advantage from it, because from his reputation for plain dealing his artifice will blind men more'.[24] This connects well to *raison d'état*.

A last word, on *raison d'état*: both Florentines can be considered to have been pioneers of the concept that state interests transcended morality.[25] They differed in how the state should preserve itself, however, in that Guicciardini was more interested in balancing the external forces, while his homologue put more emphasis on Italy needing a dictator to rally the forces against invaders.[26] We now turn to the prickly question of 'conceptual frameworks'.

CONCEPTUAL FRAMEWORKS

It is a common temptation of some international relations analysts to encase themselves in a 'conceptual framework', in the belief that they can then express what they want relevantly. They therefore enjoy model-building, cherry picking among the history books to prove their hypotheses, while the historian does not have to prove his relevance, given that all centuries are, in Ranke's words, 'equal in the eyes of God'. Just as some public relations pundits, in their quest for academic respectability, claim that the Bible, particularly the story of Peter and Paul, is an example of early public relations,[27] so some international relations realists latch onto, and re-interpret, Machiavelli, Hobbes and Thucydides, in order to promote their theories of power politics, which more often than not involve promoting unilateral war, on the primitive 'might is right principle'. They often make the error of interpreting past accounts according to their own agenda, rather than understanding the habits, customs and traditions of past eras. One recent example is that of British Prime Minister Boris Johnson's being portrayed as a Churchillian figure in his Brexit battle with Brussels. This is simply abusing and twisting history, as if the last world war and Brexit are similar events. It can reflect crooked thinking, just as some theoreticians exploit Marx to explain particular courses of action, forgetting however that Marx himself did not foresee the clash between Bolsheviks and Mensheviks, and between Trotskyists and Stalinists, all of whom were influenced by his writings. Another example of the abuse of history is that of a US government adviser writing: 'the Continental powers waited until Hitler invaded Poland in 1939[28] and America waited until after September 11 to go after Osama bin Laden [...] what risks do we run if Saddam is left in power and continues to build his arsenal.?' To compare the invasion of Poland with 9/11 betrays crooked thinking and shows how the abuse of history is a propaganda tool.

Paradoxically, many theorists, in the name of free thinking, actually demonstrate, albeit unknowingly, the antithesis of free thinking. For example, Samuel Huntingdon,[29] through his simplistic 'clash of civilisations'—knowingly or otherwise—drove herds of naïve students and politicians into a state of wishful thinking, where they expected, and therefore planned for, war. Similarly, Fukuyama, realising later the weakness of his 'end of history' theory, then decided that the answer to understanding the world's problems lay in 'masculine values and biology', writing that 'female chimps have relationships, while male chimps practise *Realpolitik*'.[30] This is simplistic and one cannot imagine the likes of Guicciardini being so dilettante. An excess of theory can addle the brain and therefore undermine the clarity and simplicity so necessary to detached understanding.[31] According to one expert, international relations theory unhelpfully reduces complex realities to monocausal explanations.[32] Many theories, often clashing with each other, are based on the particular ideology of their inventors and promoters and, when interpreted literally, and then applied willy-nilly as 'ideal models', clash with human reality, causing strife. As we shall see below, Guicciardini understood the gap between theory and practice.[33] Many theories are Procrustean, in the sense that their inventors either stretch or cut off the extremities, so that their data fit the model. Some theorists and their political servants believe that their ideal can be imposed on humanity, oblivious to the fact that perfection cannot be achieved in our world, as Guicciardini well knew. Herewith one of his most pertinent comments: 'To pronounce absolutely, categorically, and, as it were, by the card, concerning the things of this world, were a great mistake; for nearly all of them are marked by some singularity or exceptional quality due to difference in their circumstances, making it impossible to refer them all to the same standard. These differences and distinctions will not be found set forth in books, but must be taught by discretion'.[34] He elaborates yet more pertinently later: 'If it were to be wished that we could do things, or cause them to be done, exactly to our minds, and so that they should be free from the least flaw or defect. But since this were hard of accomplishment, it is a mistake to spend much time in over-refining; for opportunities will often escape you while you labour to attain perfection. And even when you think you have succeeded in your efforts, you see afterwards that you have been deceived; for such is the nature of the things of this world, that it is scarce possible to find anything which has not somewhere imperfection or blemish. We must therefore be content to take things as they are, and to reckon the least evil as a good'.[35]

A theory can however be useful as a thought-provoker. A political ideology, on the other hand, can limit detached analysis. Some years ago, a heavyweight academic seminar entitled 'Are Dialogue and Synthesis Possible in International Relations?', was unable to come to a simple answer; part of its conclusions read: 'Historically, international relations as a discipline has come to view dialogue and synthesis as incompatible objectives. [...] As a community of scholars, however, we are equally compelled to compete, - an important reason why we prefer debate over dialogue and pluralism over synthesis'. Why dialogue and synthesis should even be labelled 'objectives' strikes me as jejune, just as 'preferring debate over dialogue' lacks clear meaning, particularly since the two, not entirely easy to describe, are in any case inextricably interlinked.[36] At any event, apart from the marked difference in approach between behaviouralists and realists, the subject of international relations has been enriched—but also confused—by modernisation theory, structuralism, dependency theory, world systems analysis, positivism, constructivism, normative theory, pluralism, functionalism, game theory and various subdivisions of all these, most of which detract from each other, as well as connect in various instances. Think of a maelstrom of Venn diagrams, overlapping and clashing, with no clarity. Behind this plethora of categories lies ideology, often Marxist, with its various 'schools' (Frankfurt et al.), or 'liberal' (Chicago/neo-con et al.), these latter two laden with various internal contradictions. Hence the need for simplicity, through hard study of documents, without the seductive but mentally weakening cocktail of ideologies and models to help alleged experts hide in grand-sounding but often otiose categorisations and bromides. Guicciardini helps.

All that being said, some theories can be useful as a starting point in grasping the complexities of relations between states. Functionalism, for example, emphasises the importance of international co-operation, something that tends to be played down by extreme realists. If everybody pursued functionalism, then the world would be a peaceful place; but people are not like that. Like some other theories, it can tend towards idealism. We shall look at some theories a little more closely in Chapter Three. The aim is not to attack various theories, but rather to show that they are insufficient in coming to a clear understanding of relations between states.

There are those who advocate the importance of 'thinking outside the box' (see Prologue) to be truly free and critical in one's thinking. Yet these very advocates depend on the box, if only to escape from it. Thus their thinking is enslaved by the presence of the box, even if they claim to be unaffected by its rules and conventions: their thinking is predicated on reacting to the contents of the box. My approach is that there is no box at all to identify and then escape from.

One reason for the convoluted plethora of ideas and muddled thinking that emerge from so many theorists' attempts to explain their worldview may reflect a fear of simplicity, of mental nudity, so to speak: thus, they tend to categorise and define, in order to encapsulate their thinking in allegedly neat models. Yet these models can themselves be their self-constructed prison; the more they need to categorise, the lazier the mind can become. They shy away from simplicity, since the deep and hard scrutiny of past events is not their priority. For them, simplicity is nudity, which they fear, as they feel vulnerable. Oscar Wilde explains it better than I can, with his *dictum* that most people are other people, their thoughts being someone else's opinions, their lives a mimicry and their passions a quotation.[37] Guicciardini touches on this; let us repeat his thinking above: '[…] it is a mistake to spend much time in over-refining; for opportunities will often escape you while you labour to attain perfection. And even when you think you have succeeded in your efforts, you see afterwards that you have been deceived; for such is the nature of the things of this world, that it is scarce possible to find anything which has not somewhere imperfection or blemish. We must therefore be content to take things as they are, and to reckon the least evil as a good'.[38]

Conclusions

With a detached theory- and ideology-free study and scrutiny of history, particularly through original documents, we can begin to understand Guicciardini. The purist historian will rely essentially on verifiable documents, acting like a detective, ascertaining not only the veracity of the documents, but why they were written in the first place. Were they written to please a political master? Were they propagandistic? How accurate were they? Did they omit significant facts? Did they exaggerate? What was the motive for writing them? In his histories of Italy and Florence, Guicciardini is well known for having been one of the first people to recognise that official documents were vital in even beginning to understand a story.

History is often exploited by propagandists as a political weapon. Numerous examples abound: for example, the exaggerated demonisation of King Richard III by the Tudors (thanks to a large extent to William Shakespeare, who was beholden to Queen Elisabeth), and, more recently, the depiction of anti-communist fighters in the Greek civil war as defenders of democracy, when in fact many of them had been in the German-inspired 'security battalions', collaborating with the occupation government, but then freed from prison to kill anything that hinted at being 'left-wing'.[39]

To conclude my introduction and summarise the mental underpinning of this book, I ask you to consider this: in order to reflect, you need the space not to be forced to think. Let us now turn to Francesco Guicciardini himself.

Notes

1. My own interpretation of various translations.
2. Guicciardini, Francesco, *Counsels and Reflections*, translated from the Italian (*Ricordi Politici e Civili*) by Ninian Hill Thomson, M.A., Kegan Paul, Trench Trübner & Co., Ltd., London, 1890.
3. I believed that I had first coined the term 'geohistory', until I trawled the Internet, and found that it already existed. Two precise definitions were: 'The geological history of the Earth or of a region; history as studied in the context of geography or the earth sciences'. I found only one serious paper on the term, in the form of a paper by Jose Luis Orella Unzué of the University of San Sebastian, written in 1995. Perhaps because of the hegemonolingual situation of English, and the fact that the paper is in Spanish, it does not appear to have had any great impact on current international relations thinking. His approach differs from mine, in that his paper concludes that geohistory is a new geography. Thus his emphasis appears to be on geography, whereas mine is on history, and puts the emphasis on people's characteristics and behaviour. See *Lurralde*, no. 18, San Sebastian, 1995, ISSN 1697-3070.
4. The terms 'power politics' and 'political realism' are usually treated as one and the same. Although many political realists believe that human behaviour determines the state of the world, they tend to justify this by emphasising state power as vital to control anarchy, at an international level. This amounts to a geopolitical approach, which tries to justify the acquiring of resources (especially oil) to increase the power of the state. This can lead, and has led, to war. As we shall see towards the end of this book, my theory-free geohistory differs, in that it does not justify

grabbing other people's resources, but rather advocates the understanding of history, so as to remedy, rather than repeat, mistakes.
5. Hill, Christopher, *The Changing Politics of Foreign Policy*, Palgrave Macmillan, Basingstoke, 2003, p. 133.
6. Strauss, Leo, 'Niccolò Machiavelli', in Strauss, Leo and Cropsey, Joseph (eds.), *History of Political Philosophy*, University of Chicago, 1987 (first published in 1963), p. 297. In this book, there is a chapter on Machiavelli, but not on Guicciardini. The latter is not referred to.
7. Platias, Athanassios G., and Koliopoulos, Constantinos, *Thucydides on Strategy*, Hurst and Company, London, 2010. See my review of the book in *Journal of Global Analysis*, vol. 3, no. 1.
8. Thucydides, *History of the Peloponnesian War*, translated by Rex Warner, introduction and notes by M. I. Finlay, Penguin Books, London etc., 1972., p. 48.
9. Former US Secretary of State.
10. Mallinson, William, *Kissinger and the Invasion of Cyprus: Diplomacy in the Eastern Mediterranean*, Cambridge Scholars Publishing, Newcastle upon Tyne, 2016 and 2017, p. 2. Kissinger distinguishes between Kautilya's *Arthashastra* and Machiavelli's *The Prince*, alluding to Max Weber's comment that the former exemplified truly radical Machiavellianism, and that *The Prince* was harmless compared to it. See Kissinger, Henry, *World Order*, Allen Lane, 2014, p. 199.
11. Op. cit., Thucydides, p. 80.
12. Ibid., p. 49.
13. Ibid., p. 243.
14. Ibid., p. 245.
15. Machiavelli, Niccolò, *The Prince*, Oxford University Press, 1990, p. 84.
16. Op. cit., Guicciardini, 30, p. 18.
17. Op. cit., Guicciardini, 86, p. 41.
18. See Pocock, J.G.A. (Johns Hopkins University), 'Machiavelli and Guicciardini: Ancients and Moderns', *Canadian Journal of Political and Social Theory/Revue Canadienne de théorie politique et sociale*, Vol. 2, No., 3 (Fall/Automne 1978), for a thoughtful comparison.
19. Ibid., 236, p. 104.
20. Op. cit., Machiavelli, p. 87.
21. Ibid., p. 56.
22. Op. cit., Guicciardini, 341, p. 143.
23. Op. cit., Machiavelli, p. 59.
24. Op. cit., Guicciardini, 104, pp. 47–48.
25. See, for example, Bull, Hedley, 'Society and Anarchy in International Relations', in Butterfield, Herbert and Wight, Martin, (eds.) *Diplomatic Investigations*, George Allen & Unwin Ltd., London, 1966, p. 37.
26. Ibid., Butterfield, H., 'The Balance of Power', p. 134.

27. Grunig, James E. and Hunt, Todd (1984), *Managing Public Relations*, New York: Holt, Rinehart and Winston, p. 15.
28. Perle, Richard, 'Iraq: Saddam unbound', in Kagan, Robert and Kristol, William, *Present dangers* (San Francisco, Encounter Books, 2000P), in Dunn, David Hastings, 'Myths, motivations and 'misunderestimations,', *International Affairs*, vol. 79, no. 2, March 2003.
29. Mallinson, William, 'Does the West Exist? Huntingdon Revisited', in *Images in Words: Only History Exists*, Cambridge Scholars Publishing, Newcastle upon Tyne, 2018, 2019, pp. 34–37.
30. See Bell, Duncan, 'Beware of False Prophets: Biology, Human Nature and the Future of International Relations Theory', *International Affairs*, Vol. 82, No. 3, Chatham House, London, May, 2006, in Mallinson William, *Cyprus: Diplomatic History and the Clash of Theory in International Relations*, I. B. Tauris, London and New York, 2010.
31. For a critical analysis and evaluation of International Relations theories, see Chapter Two of op. cit., Mallinson, William, *Cyprus: Diplomatic History* etc.
32. See Professor Beatrice Heuser's review of op. cit., *The Threat of Geopolitics to International Relations*, in *International Affairs*, vol. 93, no. 3, 2017.
33. He wrote: 'How Wide the Difference Between Theory and Practice.' Op. cit., Guicciardini, 35, pp. 21–22.
34. Ibid., 6, pp. 7–8.
35. Ibid., 126, pp. 56–57.
36. Hellman, Gunther (ed.), 'Are Dialogue and Synthesis Possible in International Relations?', *International Studies Review*, Blackwell, Malden (USA), and Oxford, 2003, pp. 123–153.
37. Wilde, Oscar, 'De Profundis', *The Works of Oscar Wilde*, Collins, London, 1948.
38. Op. cit., Guicciardini, 126, pp. 56–57.
39. Mallinson, William, *Thrice a Stranger*, Cambridge Scholars Publishing, Newcastle upon Tyne, 2016, 2017, pp. 79–88.

Bibliography

Bell, Duncan, 'Beware of False Prophets: Biology, Human Nature and the Future of International Relations Theory',*International Affairs*, Vol. 82, No. 3, Chatham House, London, May, 2006.

Bull, Hedley, 'Society and Anarchy in International Relations', in Butterfield, Herbert and Wight, Martin, (eds.) *Diplomatic Investigations*, George Allen & Unwin Ltd., London, 1966.

Dunn, David Hastings, 'Myths, Motivations and 'Misunderestimations'', *International Affairs*, vol. 79, no. 2, March 2003.

Guicciardini, Francesco, *Counsels and Reflections*, translated from the Italian (*Ricordi Politici e Civili*) by Ninian Hill Thomson, M.A., Kegan Paul, Trench Trübner & Co., Ltd., London, 1890.

Grunig, James E. and Hunt, Todd, *Managing Public Relations*, New York: Holt, Rinehart and Winston, 1984.

Hellman, Gunther (ed.), 'Are Dialogue and Synthesis Possible in International Relations?', *International Studies Review*, Blackwell, Malden (USA), and Oxford, 2003.

Hill, Christopher, *The Changing Politics of Foreign Policy*, Palgrave Macmillan, Basingstoke, 2003.

Kissinger, Henry, *World Order*, Allen Lane, 2014.

Lurralde, no. 18, San Sebastian, 1995, ISSN 1697–3070.

Machiavelli, Niccolò, *The Prince*, Oxford University Press, 1990.

Mallinson, William, *Kissinger and the Invasion of Cyprus: Diplomacy in the Eastern Mediterranean*, Cambridge Scholars Publishing, Newcastle upon Tyne, 2016 and 2017.

Mallinson William, *Cyprus: Diplomatic History and the Clash of Theory International Relations*, I. B. Tauris, London and New York, 2010.

Mallinson, William, *Thrice a Stranger*, Cambridge Scholars Publishing, Newcastle upon Tyne, 2016, 2017.

Mallinson, William, *Images in Words: Only History Exists*, Cambridge Scholars Publishing, Newcastle upon Tyne, 2018, 2019.

Platias, Athanassios G., and Koliopoulos, Constantinos, *Thucydides on Strategy*, Hurst and Company, London, 2010.

Pocock, J.G.A. (Johns Hopkins University), 'Machiavelli and Guicciardini: Ancients and Moderns', *Canadian Journal of Political and Social Theory/Revue Canadienne de théorie politique et sociale*, Vol. 2, No., 3 (Fall/Automne 1978).

Strauss, Leo and Cropsey, Joseph (eds.), *History of Political Philosophy*, University of Chicago, 1987 (first published in 1963).

Thucydides, *History of the Peloponnesian War*, translated by Rex Warner, introduction and notes by M. I. Finlay, Penguin Books, London etc., 1972.

Wilde, Oscar, 'De Profundis', *The Works of Oscar Wilde*, Collins, London, 1948.

CHAPTER 2

Who Is Guicciardini?

Abstract The chapter will give an overview of Guicciardini, differentiating him from Machiavelli, and connecting some of his thinking to Thucydides. It will display through quotes from the *Ricordi* his expertise in understanding human nature; how he appears to base much of his approach on this; his understanding of the difference between theory and practice; and the importance of taking the unplanned into account. The chapter will begin to explain how history repeats itself, but in new disguises, using the example of British-Russian relations and of the tendency of former empires to continue colonialism in different ways.

Keywords Thucydides · Human nature · Theory and practice · Colonialism

> Something can be grasped better, if considered over time.[1]
> Aristotle

INTRODUCTION

Francesco Guicciardini was certainly no political ideologue, needing no rationality to prove any theory. In an age before theories and their controlling ideologies came to the fore in international relations studies, he was a statesman, diplomat and historian, working at a time when Italian art was head and shoulders above that of the rest of Europe, despite the political chaos and foreign interference in Italy's affairs that so irritated his more hard-headed but highly intelligent homologue Niccolò Machiavelli. His professional *raison d'être* was to ensure the survival and strength of Florence, at a time of treachery, power-lust and skullduggery. One respected modern authority writes that Guicciardini—and Machiavelli—represents the crude beginnings of what might be called the science of international politics,[2] which we shall deal with in the following chapter. Some of the positions that he held during his career were those of lawyer, ambassador (he was definitely a high-flyer, being appointed ambassador to the court of the King of Aragon at the age of twenty-nine), Governor of Reggio, Modena and Parma, the province of Romagna, and Lieutenant-General of the papal armies. An early version of the quintessential powerful civil servant *par excellence,* he managed to hang on to power until he was dismissed by Cosimo de Medici (whom he had nevertheless helped to rise to power), spending his last three years writing. Unlike Machiavelli, he managed to 'retire' without being tortured. But today, he is best known as a historian, in particular for his histories of Italy and of Florence, and for his use of government sources to support arguments, along with his realistic analysis of the people and events of his time. He also had an acerbic sense of humour, describing, for example, Cardinal Passerini as 'a eunuch who spent the whole day in idle chatter, neglecting important things'.[3]

According to one Italian patriot, Machiavelli respected his homologue Guicciardini, to the point of adoration. 'I love Messer Guicciardini'.[4] He continues, '[...] Even Machiavelli, whose name has been proverbial as that of the heartless codifier of the Italian rules of the game, paid homage to his rival, for whom he felt not only the highest esteem, a rare sentiment among competitors, but also admiration, friendship, and even love. [...] The two men have been compared repeatedly through the centuries. The parallel is almost irresistible. After all, they were both Florentines, born in the same city at about the same time (Machiavelli in 1469 and Guicciardini in 1482); both started young, when the popular republic of Florence employed them as ambassadors; both pursued government careers, and were fascinated by the technique of governing men and achieving power'.[5]

But there the direct comparison ends. Although both men separated their private and moral life from affairs of state and were undoubtedly pragmatic in outlook, Machiavelli appears in his writing as the more emotional and indignant of the two, while Guicciardini was more circumspect. For example, unlike Machiavelli's apparent belief in a strong, even dictatorial, Italy, Guicciardini believed that if you were strong, neutrality was a good option.[6] It was better to avoid the fray, and play, where possible, a balancing act.[7] As regards Machiavelli's well-known justification for cruelty (when necessary to preserve the power of a prince), this reflects a more pessimistic view of human nature than that held by Guicciardini. Nevertheless, in his professional life, Guicciardini was not averse to condoning a spot of skullduggery: when Alessandro, Duke of Florence, was assassinated in his bed, Guicciardini agreed that the murder should be kept secret.[8] At any event, in treacherous times, Guicciardini, as well as Machiavelli, was a survivor who kept his private opinions to himself. He despised hypocrisy, corruption and tyranny, yet was obliged in public life to live with them, and even condone them. His *forte* was surely his perceptiveness of human nature and his concomitant understanding of human characteristics, and therefore of the vagaries of human behaviour. Let us now briefly consider this.

HUMAN CHARACTERISTICS AND BEHAVIOUR

At this point, we need to understand that Guicciardini was well trained in the Classics. Much of his evaluation of human character can be linked to Aristotle's *The Art of Rhetoric*, in which the latter analyses the characteristics of different types of people.[9] And as regards Greek historians, his analyses are strikingly similar to Thucydides' views on power relationships between Greek city states. It was indeed the Renaissance's re-discovery of ancient Greek literature and culture which stimulated educated men such as Guicciardini and Machiavelli. Guicciardini was certainly no starry-eyed ideologue, just as Thucydides was not. Both men lived at a time when both Italy and Greece were undergoing a strong dose of chaos, with wars between city states, shifting alliances, and the involvement of strong external powers: France, the Holy Roman Empire and Spain, in the case of Italy, and the Persian Empire in the case of Greece. Both saw human nature and characteristics as vital, if not essential, causes of events. Guicciardini's understanding of human nature can be encapsulated in this maxim of his: 'How wide the difference between theory and practice, and how many there are who, with abundant knowledge, remember not or know not how to turn it to account! [...]'[10] Such words meant that even those who disliked Guicciardini respected his wisdom. For example, Benedetto Varchi,[11] for all his alleged hatred[12] of Guicciardini, wrote: 'Messer Francesco, besides his wealth, his degree of knowledge, besides being governor or lieutenant of the Pope, was also famous for the practical knowledge he possessed of human actions, which he discussed and judged with great perception'.[13] To try and understand his perceptiveness, Guicciardini's own words begin to enlighten us: 'Everybody likes open, truthful and frank persons. To be open, truthful and frank is a noble and generous thing, although often harmful. On the other hand, dissimulation and deception are useful and often indispensable, because of the evil nature of men. These arts are, however, despised and hated by everybody. Therefore I do not know which behaviour to choose. I would suggest truthfulness to be ordinarily preferred, without abandoning deception altogether. That is, in the ordinary circumstances of life, use truthfulness in such a way as to gain the reputation of a guileless man. In a few important cases, use deceit. Deceit is the more fruitful and successful the more you enjoy the reputation of an honest and truthful man; you are more easily believed'.[14]

He then qualifies this perceptive and frank view with: 'Those men conduct their affairs well who keep in front of their eyes their ówn private interest and measure all their actions according to its necessities. [...] Unfortunately too many short-sighted men think that their interest lies mainly in the accumulation of wealth and not also in keeping a good reputation and a good name'.[15] We see in both these quotes Guicciardini's understanding of the difference between ideal behaviour and reality: 'How wide the difference between theory and practice!' (see above).

Bearing in mind Shakespeare's quote 'All that glisters is not gold',[16] we can repeat Guicciardini's *dictum*: 'Since a name for goodness will help you in numberless ways, do all you can to seem good. But since false appearances are never lasting, you can hardly succeed in seeming good for long, unless you be so in reality'.[17]

Whether they know it or not, most people tend to engage in a measure of subtle rhetoric, if not persuasion, when talking to others, or even to oneself. One priest *cum* public relations entrepreneur got close to admitting it when he began an address to public relations practitioners and educationalists with the words: 'We all lie a bit'.[18] The audience sniggered knowingly.

Apart from human nature per se (and not everyone agrees on what exactly human nature is), it is the behaviour emanating from human nature that determines the state of the world, behaviour that can be unpredictable, according to Guicciardini. This commonsense observation is however often ignored. Human nature can lead to good as well as bad acts, but the tendency of out and out realists is to assume the worst and, therefore to plan for the worst, something which Guicciardini does not propose. As we shall see by the end of this book, moderate classical realism (which connects with parts of the English School,[19] which had its heyday in the Sixties) approaches some of Guicciardini's thinking. Guicciardini seems to have predicated much of his thought on a measure of cautious optimism: 'All men are by nature more inclined to good than to evil; nor is there anyone who, when other considerations do move him to the contrary, would not willingly do you a benefit than an injury. But human nature is so frail, and open to so many temptations, that men easily allow themselves to deviate from their natural goodness'.[20] Giuicciardini's more optimistic circumspection contrasts with Machiavelli's harsher view: 'For one can generally say this about men: they are ungrateful, fickle, simulators and deceivers, avoiders of danger, greedy for gain'.[21] Here one can but wonder whether Machiavelli's experience of being tortured and then forced to retire may have embittered some of his writing. In a relevant aside, let us remember that Thomas Hobbes, writing over one hundred years later, described Man's life as solitary, poor, nasty, brutish and short.

At any event, we see in Guicciardini's assessment of human nature a flash of Thucydides, who wrote: 'Love of power, operating through greed and through personal ambition, was the cause of all this evil'.[22] Guicciardini enhances this by writing: 'For greedy men believe easily whatsoever they desire'.[23] 'Avarice in a prince is incomparably more hateful than in a private man'.[24] 'I believe that, all things considered, greater results are to be obtained by moderation and patience than by impetuosity and daring'.[25] This contrasts with some of Machiavelli's more aggressive thinking about the use of power. Guicciardini, while not eschewing war, is less rumbustious than the former: 'Wars have no greater peril than he who has just entered upon them should take their success for certain'.[26] 'Accordingly there is nothing more ruinous than to enter on a campaign when you are without ready money, and have to pay by drafts at long dates; for in this way you rather feed the war than finish it'.[27] We can glean from this that his thinking is based on a considerable degree of circumspection. There is no shooting from the hip.

Guicciardini's History

To understand Guicciardini's astuteness as a historian and statesman, let us again quote from Luigi Barzini's book, *The Italians*. He begins his book with one of Guicciardini's *dicta*, taken in turn from *I Ricordi*: 'Past things shed light on future ones; the world was always of a kind; what is and will be was at some other time; the same things come back, but under different names and colours; not everybody recognizes them, but only he who is wise and considers them diligently'.[28] Here we can quote Thucydides more fully (see above), since we see the same wise thinking: 'And it may well be that my history will seem less easy to read because of the absence in it of a romantic element. It will enough for me, however, if these words of mine are judged useful by those who want to understand clearly the events which happened in the past and which (human nature being what it is) will, at some time or other and in much the same ways, be repeated in the future. My work is not a piece of writing designed to meet the taste of an immediate public, but was done to last forever'.[29] It is still being published today, serving as a 'bible' for serious historians.

The work for which Guicciardini is most remembered, however, is *History of Italy*,[30] where he shows his *penchant* towards democratic rule in Ancient Greece. His conclusions, according to Strathern, 'have the seasoned insight one would expect of a man who had served as an ambassador, had been the closest councillor of two popes (Leo X and Clement VII) and had advised two rulers (Alessandro and Cosimo). As such, his History of Florence is not only more reliable but superior in judgment to that produced by Machiavelli, his earlier contemporary. Guicciardini was not entirely scrupulous, either in his life or in his *History*, but his advice (and his writing) was not Machiavellian'.[31] Thus, while Machiavelli is adored by many out and out political realists for his justification of force in the interests of the state, the same cannot be said for Guicciardini, who comes across as more moderate.

Guicciardini clearly thinks that human behaviour, for all its quirks and unpredictability, is the essential factor in understanding how states function, and that this is why history is a constant repetition of events, distinguished only by new names and colours. Let us look at a few topics to test the validity of his contention. An obvious one is Britain's traditional fear of Russia and concomitant support of the Ottoman Empire. As early as 1791, William Pitt the Younger denounced Russia for its supposed ambitions to dismember Turkey.[32] By the time of Napoleon's defeat,

Britain was focusing on Russia as the main hindrance to its wish to control the Eastern Mediterranean. It is no exaggeration to say that throughout the whole of the nineteenth century, one of the British Empire's main preoccupations was with Russia, owing to the latter's usually hostile attitude towards the Ottoman Empire. This fixation became such a habit, that it transcended mere national interests. The obsession with Russia also explains Britain's relations with Greece: a myth abounds that in 1832, a new and sovereign monarchical Greece was created. Sovereign it was, up to a point, but as a protectorate of the major powers, the very powers involved in agreeing to its existence. Let us look briefly at how this came about: by the time of the struggle for Greek independence, Greece had become a mere geohistorical tool of the British Empire, the latter even owning some Greek lands, the Ionian Islands. It is to Russia, not Britain, that Greece owes its qualified freedom (although revolutionary and Napoleonic France also have an intellectual claim), and it was despite, not because of, Britain, that the 1821 revolution ended in independence. It was the Anglo-Russian Protocol of 4 April 1826 that led to some of Greece being freed from the Ottomans: it stated that Britain would mediate to make Greece an autonomous vassal of the Ottoman Empire, but that if this proved impossible, Britain or Russia could intervene jointly or *separately*. Russia intervened, and by 1828, Greece, or at least some of it, was free, under the pro-Russian Capodistrias, although after his murder in 1831 by two pro-British brothers, it was then declared a protectorate of Britain, France and Russia, under a Bavarian king. When the philhellenic Admiral Codrington and his French and Russian homologues had sunk the Egyptian-Ottoman fleet at Navarino, the Foreign Secretary, Wellington, is well known for having described the battle, in typical English understatement, as an 'untoward event', while his ally Metternich described it as a 'dreadful catastrophe'. Somewhat arrogantly and cynically, the latter had also, when speaking of the Greeks, said: 'Over there, beyond our frontiers, three or four hundred thousand individuals hanged, impaled, or with their throats cut, hardly count'.[33] Needless to say, Metternich disliked Capodistrias.

Whatever the protestations of well-paid off designer academics in both Britain and Greece, British policy has been essentially antithetical to Greek interests since the very inception of the modern Greek state, mainly because of her support for the Ottoman Empire and now Turkey as a bulwark against Russia. In Guicciardini's eyes, the same things return.

In 1841, the British minister (ambassador) to Greece, Edmund Lyons, said: 'A truly independent Greece is an absurdity. Greece can either be English or Russian, and since she must not be Russian, it is necessary that she be English'.[34]

Apart from a few flashes in the pan, and a few individuals like Canning, the only help Greece has received has been from private individuals such as Lord Byron or public individuals who were brave enough to go against official British policy, such as Admiral Codrington. Britain was forced into helping Greece, to keep a finger in the Mediterranean pie, for fear of Russia ending up as Greece's main sponsor, and weakening Britain's Ottoman friends. The Don Pacifico Affair is a good example of Britain's attitude, when Britain actually threatened Greece with gunboats, while during the Crimean War, Britain, with its then French aides, blockaded Piraeus. In 1916, Britain and France even interfered militarily in Greece, being beaten back by the King's forces, then getting their revenge by backing the controversial and Lloyd George-friendly Venizelos, who favoured war: he led Greece into a war which was to lead to the famous catastrophe of over one million Ottoman citizens of Greek stock being expelled from their birthplace, with many murdered on the way out.

The next war is another example of the continuity of Britain's approach, as Guicciardini would surely agree: Britain, having supported the strongest anti-German resistance, ELAS,[35] then turned against it, ending up supporting those Greek forces which had been closest to the German occupiers, and fuelling a destructive civil war, essentially because of her obsession with Russia. As Francis Noel-Baker wrote: 'Instead of making Greek resistance more moderate, more democratic, more truly representative of the mass of Greek opinion, we drove it to extremes'.[36]

Extracts from a Foreign Office (FCO) paper prepared for the Foreign Minister, Anthony Eden, in June 1944, show how Britain betrayed her main anti-German Greek resistance allies, essentially because of her obsession with, and distrust of, the Soviet Union (which was for them Russia): '[...] Nor can any accusation be levelled against the Russians of organising the spread of communism in the Balkans.[...] The Soviet Government's support of the Communist-led elements in these countries is not so much based on ideological grounds as on the fact that such elements are most responsive to and are the most vigorous in resisting the axis.[...] Furthermore, if anyone is to blame for the present situation in which the Communist-led movements are the most powerful elements in Yugoslavia and Greece, it is we ourselves. Russia's historical interest in the Balkans has always manifested itself in a determination that no other Great Power shall dominate them, as this would constitute a strategical threat to Russia. [...] whereas in the nineteenth century we had Austro-Hungary as an ally to counter these Russian measures there is no one on whom we can count to support us this time. [...] As a result of our approach to the Soviet Government, however, the latter have now agreed to let us take the lead in Greece'.[37]

Apart from the clear evidence that the British fixation with Russia (and her oxymoronic support for the communists in Yugoslavia and the anti-communists in Greece) and the Eastern Mediterranean had not changed (and continues at the time of writing), we see here that Churchill's and Stalin's 'percentages agreement' at Yalta a few months later, whereby Greece would be ten per cent Russian and ninety per cent English, already existed. Greece was merely a geopolitical tool for Britain, which was soon to replace Austro-Hungary with the US to counter the Soviet Union. Some of the main ingredients of the Greek civil war were Churchill's obsession with the return of an unpopular Greek king,[38] Britain's obsession with Russia, and thus the way in which Britain helped, whether by default or design, to polarise the forces in Greece. In this sense, the Cold War began in the Balkans since, as we can see, the Foreign Office (FO) was already doing its utmost to keep the Soviet Union well away from Greece, well before the struggle for Germany had begun. Indeed, the Allies had only just landed in Normandy. The Joint Planning Staff wrote in December 1945: 'Our strategic interest is to ensure that no unfriendly power, by the acquisition of Greek bases, can threaten our Mediterranean communications. On the other hand, we wish to liquidate our present military commitment as soon as possible'.[39]

In 1947, Britain handed Greece to America, thus introducing US and future NATO power into the Balkans. The Truman Doctrine and massive deliveries of military hardware—as well as the Tito-Stalin disagreement—put an end to the civil war by 1949, and a bitter and exhausted Greece joined NATO in 1952. But the divisions caused by the civil war lived on in the Greek party-political system. Shades of it still exist today. Britain's hanging onto its bases in Cyprus, under American pressure to do so, is part and parcel of its continuing concern with Russia. In 1975, the FCO wrote: 'We must also recognise that in the final analysis Turkey must be regarded as more important to Western strategic interests than Greece and that, if risks must be run, they should be risks of further straining Greek rather than Turkish relations with the West'.[40] Today, Britain continues to hang onto its bases in Cyprus, having succumbed to American pressure to keep them, and its nineteenth century concern about, and hostility towards, Russia is in full swing. To put matters simply, one could argue that, based on the evidence, the same human characteristics, individual and corporate, are always present, sometimes dormant for a while, yet inevitably awakening, in line with Guicciardini's perspective.

Other examples of Giuicciardini's thinking about the same things returning with new names and colours are Turkey's current 'neo-Ottomanism', which includes expansionist claims on Greek territory; American interference in South America; British (more traditionally English) attempts to undermine the creation of a strong Europe with its own army independent of NATO, an attitude that has its origins in Henry VIII's break from Rome, and in England's and then Britain's subsequent involvement in Europe's wars; and, more generally, what could be termed 'post-imperial *rigor mortis*', namely the tendency of past empires to involve themselves in their past possessions. Here, French military activity in certain African countries comes to mind. A more recent case is that of the behaviour of the authorities in some countries during the COVID lockdowns, which has given rise to suggestions that the world is returning to the dictatorial regimes of the Thirties: for example, a German doctor critical of the lockdowns was brutally arrested at home in November 2020 by armed police while broadcasting on YouTube, giving rise to criticisms that the authorities are behaving like the Gestapo.[41] Or perhaps it is simply that the same age-old human characteristics manifest themselves from time to time, depending on circumstances which, as Guicciardini notes, can be unpredictable.

Fortune

Given his scepticism about trying to achieve perfection, and his belief that theory does not correspond to practice (see Chapter 1), it is hardly surprising that Guicciardini does not depend merely on rationalism, believing that fortune has a rôle to play in human affairs. He writes: 'Hence you may gather how great are the perils of conspiracy, since the measures which in other cases ensure safety here only bring danger. Another reason for this I think may be, that Fortune, which has much to say in these matters, is displeased with him who labours too strenuously to withdraw them from her control'.[42] 'A wise captain, if not constrained by necessity, will never bring his army into battle unless he see that it will fight to great advantage; for the issue is too much in the hands of Fortune, and defeat too serious a risk'.[43] 'But it is a finer thing to use this good fortune worthily: I mean by extending mercy and pardon'.[44] 'Even they who, ascribing everything to prudence and capacity, would seek to shut out Fortune, cannot deny it to be a happy chance that opportunities should at the right moment present themselves for displaying to advantage those talents or qualities wherein a man excels. For we see from experience that the same qualities are differently esteemed at different times, and that things which are pleasing if done to-day may displease if done tomorrow'.[45]

CONCLUSIONS

Who then was Francesco Guicciardini? We have seen much of his thinking above, and can see that he was a pretty shrewd character, who believed in balancing reason with fortune; who was circumspect; and who was a realistic rather than fanatical believer in power politics per se. Above all, he was an expert in understanding human nature, characteristics and behaviour. He combined ambassadorial rôles with advisory ones, and with positions of power, no mean feat.

In 1596, Ottaviano Maggi[46] contended that an ambassador should be a trained theologian, well versed in Aristotle and Plato, and able at a moment's notice to solve the most abstruse problems in correct dialectical form: he should also be expert in mathematics, architecture, music, physics and civil and canon law. He should speak and write Latin fluently and must also be proficient in Greek, Spanish, French, German and Turkish. While being a trained classical scholar, a historian, a geographer and an expert in military science, he must also have a cultured taste for poetry. And above all, he must be of excellent family, rich and endowed with a fine physical presence.[47] Guicciardini was most of these things. It is probably his Classical education, as well as his having considered joining the church, that forged his understanding of the difference between private morality and public realism, when morals sometimes had to take a back seat. But apart from his realisticness, Guicciardini was the very antithesis of a pedant, as the following shows: 'You cannot adhere always to one fixed and unbending rule; so that if it be often disadvantageous to be too open in your talk even with friends - I mean in matters which should be kept secret – on the other hand to let your friends perceive that you are keeping something from them is a sure way to make them do the like by you. For since nothing gains you another's confidence so much as his belief that you confide in him, your reticence towards others may deprive you of opportunities of learning from them. Here, therefore, as in so many other cases, the character of men, of times, and of circumstances has to be taken into account. To this end, discretion is needed, which, if it be not given us by nature, can seldom be sufficiently learned from experience, from books never'.[48] Put more incisively, he believed that the exception makes the rule. After all, without rules, could there be exceptions? Let us now turn to the musings of theoreticians, some of whom, particularly through their paradigms and models, tend to imprison themselves in pure pedantry.

NOTES

1. My own interpretation of various translations.
2. Butterfield, Herbert and Wight, Martin (eds.), *Diplomatic Investigations, Essays in the Theory of International Politics*, George Allen & Unwin Ltd., London, 1966. 'The Balance of Power', H. Butterfield, p. 133.
3. Strathern, Paul, *The Medici*, Pimlico, London, 2005, p. 308; first published by Jonathan Cape, London, 2003.
4. Barzini, Luigi, *The Italians*, Bantam Books, 1965, published by arrangement with the original publishers, Atheneum Publishers, 1964, pp. 164–5.
5. Ibid.
6. Op. cit., Butterfield, pp. 134–5.
7. Guicciardini, Francesco, *Storia d'Italia*, book One, Chapter One, in op. cit., Butterfield, p. 137.
8. Op. Cit., Strathern, p. 328.
9. Aristotle, *The Art of Rhetoric*, translated and introduced by Lawson Tancred, H. C. (1991), London: Penguin Books, pp. 178–9.
10. Guicciardini, Francesco, *Counsels and Reflections*, translated from the Italian (*Ricordi Politici e Civili*) by Ninian Hill Thomson, MA, Kegan Paul, Trench Trübner & Co., Ltd., London, 1890, 35, pp. 21–22.
11. Benedetti Varchi (1503–65) was a historian, humanist and poet. He was arrested for pederasty, but pardoned by Cosimo de Medici.
12. According to op. cit., Barzini, p. 167.
13. Ibid.
14. Ibid., p. 171.
15. Ibid.
16. From *The Merchant of Venice*.
17. Guicciardini, *Counsels and Reflections*, 44, pp. 25–6.
18. Van der Meiden, Anne (1989), *Address* to meeting of European Confederation of Public Relations, Brussels.

19. See op. cit., Butterfield, Herbert and Wight, Martin, *Diplomatic Investigations*. While some of the mainly sensible analyses and observations by the writers tend a little towards constructivism, some of their common sense does tie in with Guicciardini's ideas.
20. Op. cit., Guicciardini, 134, p. 60. Seemingly contradictorily, he writes later: '[...] there are more bad than good men in this world, and more especially wherever there comes to be a question as to property or power' (134, p. 90.) But there is nothing essentially contradictory in these two statements, since 'bad men' can still be naturally inclined towards goodness, even if they fail in being good.
21. Machiavelli, Niccolò, *The Prince*, Oxford University Press, 1990, p. 56.
22. Thucydides, *History of the Peloponnesian War*, translated by Rex Warner, introduction and notes by M. I. Finlay, Penguin Books, London etc., 1972, p. 243.
23. Op. cit., Guicciardini, 105, p. 48.
24. Ibid., 31, p. 133.
25. Op. cit., Guicciardini, 381, pp. 160–2.
26. Ibid., 180, p. 79.
27. Ibid., 149, p. 67. This has considerable relevance today. The US, for example, which attacked Iraq, allegedly to impose freedom and obliterate terrorism, spent huge sums of money. See Friedman, Uri, 'Fighting Terrorism With a Credit Card: Interest payments on America's war debt could one day exceed the direct costs of combat itself', *The Atlantic*, 12 September 2016.
28. Op. cit., Barzini, p. ix. The English wording differs slightly in op. cit., Guicciardini's *Counsels and Reflections*: 'Past events shed light on future, because the world has always been the same as it now is, and all that is now, or shall be hereafter, has been in time past. Things accordingly repeat themselves, but under changed names and colours, so that it is not everyone who can recognise them, but only he who is discerning and who notes and considers them diligently' (336, p. 141). Earlier back, Guicciardini has a slightly shortened version (27, p. 27). Whether or not this is due to repetitiveness on Guicciardini's part, or to later editing must, I think, remain a moot point.
29. Op. cit., Thucydides, p. 48.
30. Guicciardini, Francesco, *History of Italy*, republished by BiblioLife, 2009.
31. Op.cit., Strathern p. 332.
32. Wallbank, T. Walter et al. (eds.), *Civilisation, Past and Present*, volume II, Harper Collins, 1996, p. 721.
33. Sked, Alan (ed.), *Europe's Balance of Power, 1815–1848*, Macmillan, London, 1979, p. 7. Sked quotes de Bertier de Sauvigny in *Metternich and his Times*, Darton, Lonman and Todd, 1962, p. 251.

34. Clogg, Richard, *A Concise History of Greece*, Cambridge University Press, 1992, p. 57.
35. Greek People's Liberation Army.
36. Noel-Baker, Francis, *Greece: The Whole Story*, Hutchinson & Co., London, 1946, p. 43.
37. Top Secret Foreign Office Memorandum for Secretary of State, 7 June, 1944, BNA FO 371/43646, file R 9092. in Mallinson, William, *Britain and Cyprus: Key Themes and Documents since World War Two* [really World War Four, see note 13], I.B. Tauris, London and New York, 2011, pp. 12–14.
38. See Woodhouse, C.M., *The Struggle for Greece, 1941–1949*, C. Hurst and Co. Ltd., London, 2002, originally published in 1976 by Hart-Davis, MacGibbon Ltd., p. 110, where he writes : 'The combined stubbornness of Churchill and the King was the proximate cause of the tragedy'.
39. Report by Joint Planning Staff, 3 December 1945, FCO 371/48288, file R 21028/G.
40. 'British interests in the Eastern Mediterranean', *paper* prepared by Western European Department, FCO, 11 April 1975, FCO 46/1248, file DPI/516/1.
41. https://www.youtube.com/watch?v=0Ysmk80WP2M, 20 November 2020.
42. Op. cit., Guicciardini, *Ricordi*, 20, p. 12.
43. Ibid., 183, p. 81.
44. Ibid., 256, p. 110.
45. Ibid., 274, pp. 116–117.
46. A Venetian diplomat.
47. Nicolson, Harold, *Diplomacy*, Oxford University Press, 1969, p. 56.
48. Op. cit., Guicciardini, *Ricordi*, 186, pp. 82–83.

Bibliography

Aristotle, *The Art of Rhetoric*, translated and introduced by Lawson Tancred, H. C., Penguin Books, London, 1991.

Barzini, Luigi, *The Italians*, Bantam Books, 1965, published by arrangement with the original publishers, Atheneum Publishers, 1964.

Butterfield, Herbert and Wight, Martin (eds.), *Diplomatic Investigations, Essays in the Theory of International Politics*, George Allen & Unwin Ltd., London, 1966.

Clogg, Richard, *A Concise History of Greece*, Cambridge University Press, 1992.

Friedman, Uri, 'Fighting Terrorism With a Credit Card: Interest payments on America's war debt could one day exceed the direct costs of combat itself', *The Atlantic*, 12 September 2016.

Guicciardini, Francesco, *Counsels and Reflections*, translated from the Italian (*Ricordi Politici e Civili*) by Ninian Hill Thomson, MA, Kegan Paul, Trench Trübner & Co., Ltd., London, 1890.
Guicciardini, Francesco, *History of Italy*, republished by BiblioLife, 2009.
Machiavelli, Niccolò, *The Prince*, Oxford University Press, 1990.
Mallinson, William, *Britain and Cyprus: Key Themes and Documents since World War Two*, I.B. Tauris, London and New York, 2011.
Nicolson, Harold, *Diplomacy*, Oxford University Press, 1969.
Noel-Baker, Francis, *Greece: The Whole Story*, Hutchinson & Co., London, 1946.
Sked, Alan (ed.), *Europe's Balance of Power, 1815–1848*, Macmillan, London, 1979.
Strathern, Paul, *The Medici*, Pimlico, London, 2005, p. 308; first published by Jonathan Cape, London, 2003.
Thucydides, *History of the Peloponnesian War*, translated by Rex Warner, introduction and notes by M. I. Finlay, Penguin Books, London etc., 1972.
Wallbank, T. Walter et al. (eds.), *Civilisation, Past and Present*, volume II, Harper Collins, 1996.
Woodhouse, C.M., *The Struggle for Greece, 1941–1949*, C. Hurst and Co. Ltd., London, 2002, originally published in 1976 by Hart-Davis, MacGibbon Ltd.

CHAPTER 3

The War of the Theories

Abstract The chapter offers a trenchant critique of international relations theories which, while often useful as an aid to thinking about the world, tend to muddy the waters of clear understanding. While pointing to the confusion reigning in international relations theory—which reflects the current disorder in the world—and suggesting reasons for this, the chapter advocates a simpler, more reliable and less controversial method of understanding relations between states. Were it not for the very effort in trying to understand the theories considered, it would be difficult to explain geohistory, since it is the very fact that matters need clarification that leads us to geohistory as an approach.

Keywords International relations · Disorder · Geohistory · Behaviouralism · Realism

> Where is the wisdom lost to knowledge, where is the knowledge lost to information and where is the word we lost in words?[1]
>
> T. S. Eliot.

INTRODUCTION

'Man's love for words is his first step towards ignorance, and his love for definitions the second. The more he analyses, the more he has need to define, and the more he defines, the more he aims at an impossible logical perfection, for the effect of aiming at logical perfection is only a sign of ignorance'.[2] Harsh though these words may be, they nevertheless carry an underlying message that simply theorising per se through ever increasing attempts to define and sub-define to find the pot of gold at the end of the rainbow can be frustratingly fruitless. We shall aim here to briefly describe and comment on the various main international relations theories touched on in Chapter 1, bearing in mind that many of these theories were acquired from political science, having drawn on the natural sciences and also introduced normative concepts. Before we weigh in, it is important to emphasise that the aim is not to rant against international relations theories, many of which stimulate thinking, but rather to explore and identify inadequacies (Fig. 3.1).

REALISTS AND BEHAVIOURALISTS

Once upon a time, the study of international relations as a discrete subject was reasonably unpolemical. Its formal study began at the University of Aberystwyth in 1919, as a sub-discipline of international politics. Given the emotion following the death of millions in the Great War, it was approached in a hopeful, almost idealistic style. *Plus ça change*: it was not long before the theorisers put their finger in the pie, thereby politicising what could have been a tight area of study based on international history, the mechanics of diplomacy, and law. But then normative theory,[3] essentially the study of ethical values, began to politicise, so to speak, the study of international relations, which became so closely linked to international politics, as to be virtually synonymous with it. Although some of the social sciences were themselves embryonic as academic subjects when international theories were beginning to come off the American academic conveyor belt, they began to make inroads, much to the chagrin of classical realists.

Classical realism is simply a name given a posteriori to realism and emphasises the state as the key ingredient of human organisation; it postulates, perhaps rather obviously, that since human behaviour determines the state of the world (in this sense Hobbes was correct in writing that

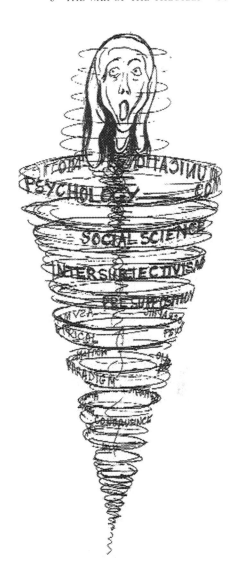

Fig. 3.1 Confusion illustration by the artist David Mallinson

Man's life was solitary, poor, nasty, brutish and short), the state and its interests are the starting point. Neorealism (or structural realism), while also seeing the state as the key ingredient of human organisation, lays more emphasis on what it considers to be the anarchy of the world, while the more neo-classical realism attempts to combine the two, by bringing in systemic pressures and the distribution of power. At a general level, the practice of out and out realism is considered to be synonymous with power politics. It is not surprising that politicians, and IR theorists themselves, sometimes get slightly confused when trying to define and sub-define, particularly since political science has infiltrated the study of international relations, increasingly affecting the theory and practice of realism. To muddy the waters a little more, many people use the term *realpolitik* as a synonym for realism, when it is in fact an approach based on achieving limited but realistic state objectives and is often used to describe and explain Bismarck's approach. At any event, it is easy to see why geopoliticians such as Henry Kissinger are attracted to realism, given the tendency of power politics towards the 'might is right' principle, and the emphasis of geopolitics on resources. Whatever the theory, the welfare of human beings takes second place to the acquisition of resources.

The behaviouralist, or social science approach, differs radically from original classical realism, in that it uses political science, sociology and psychology, but also models from the natural sciences, applying them to the study of international relations. It therefore lays itself open to the criticism of being a 'parasitic discipline', a sponge or even a sponge's sponge, given social science's use of natural science models, particularly from chemistry. It does not see the state as its starting point. Classical liberals and realists alike have attacked social science. Friedrich von Hayek, for example, considered the word 'social' to be one of those 'weasel words which drain the meaning from the concept to which they are attached', referring to the term 'social science' as the application of untested speculations to political topics,[4] while an international relations professor at the London School of Economics likened social scientists to 'peasants who believe there is a pot of gold at the end of the rainbow, despite their repeated failures to track it down'.[5] The 'English School', with its emphasis on international society, dismisses the behavioural approach of what it terms 'the American School of scientific politics'.[6]

Mental Mess

With the fall of the Berlin Wall in 1989, and the accompanying international euphoria, hard-nosed realism/power politics temporarily went backstage, giving way for a while to more idealistic views. But the harsh reality of the dark side of human behaviour did not take long to reassert itself. Rather than indulge in a bout of good old Bismarckian *Realpolitik*, the US decided that it needed to use its physical power. The writings of the likes of Leo Strauss influenced the likes of Paul Wolfowitz, one of the chief architects of the illegal war against Iraq. For all its intellectual bombast, the Strauss school of thinking, attractive to political realists and neocons, is not averse to over-interpretation and even misrepresentation in the quest for power projection, which can be a euphemism for unilateral military attacks. As mentioned in Chapter 1, even Strauss himself wrote some pretty rum things, for example that Machiavelli 'ostensibly seeks to bring about the rebirth of the ancient Roman Republic', and that he was a restorer of 'something old and forgotten',[7] whereas he simply wished to unite Italy, preferably under Florence. Even if political realists often avoid behavioural tendencies and methodologies, they tend to put words into the mouths of respected classical writers, such as Thucydides, Machiavelli and Hobbes (three key figures for political realists), as we saw in Chapter 1. Yet it is only rarely that Thucydides passes judgement. As for the argument that Thucydides believed in power politics and the use of force per se, it is equally, if not more, likely that he bewailed its use.

It must by now be clear that the relationship between political realists and behaviouralists is a mental maze at the least. The subject of international relations has been enriched or infected—depending on your point of view—by various theories, many of them overlapping and/or clashing with each other. Let us give a potted version of some of the main ones.

Structuralism lays more emphasis on overall structure than on individual states, and has influenced neorealism; modernisation theory argues that all states eventually pass through the same stages; dependency theory—which can also be considered as a sub-theory of structuralism—challenges modernisation theory's assumption that all states pass through similar stages, by emphasising the exploiter-exploited relationship; world systems analysis views the world as consisting of three categories of states: core, semi-peripheral and peripheral; positivism, a derivative of empiricism (i.e. knowledge comes from sensory experience), posits that society operates on the same criteria as the physical world; anti-positivism argues the opposite; constructivism aims to demonstrate that ideas and preferences are fundamental factors in shaping the way in which the world is organised; objectivism claims that the purpose of life is the pursuit of individual happiness, and that individual rights and *laisser-faire* capitalism are the key answer; normative theory (see above) introduces specifically moral and political content to the study of international relations: pluralism maintains that the state is only one of the elements that form the world, and thus clashes with realism's insistence that the state is the prime element; functionalism attempts to show that what really matters is international co-operation.

Let us end our admittedly potted account of some of the main theories that have characterised international relations, with post-modernism. We do this because, perhaps understandably, this body of theory, connected to critical theory, questions the fundamental assumptions of most international relations—and other—theories. It is strongly connected to the Frankfurt School, which has strong Marxist tendencies; it is also connected to deconstructivism. One difficulty of deconstructing (a euphemism for destroying) is that it is difficult to know how to replace what has been putatively destroyed. Perhaps critical readers may consider geohistory (see Chapter 6) more useful.

All the above have been flavoured with the main ideologies of conservatism, liberalism and socialism. And to further flavour an already somewhat confusing collage, we have the English School's sensible and clear categorisation of international relations thinking into three traditions: the Hobbesian, which stresses the power of sovereign will; the Grotian, which advocates the application of strong international rules in an anarchic state system; and the Kantian (much loved by extreme free-marketeers), which stresses the power of the individual, and has influenced objectivism, whose main proponent was Ayn Rand, an anti-Communist immigrant to America. Guicciardini would surely snigger at much of the above, bar the English School, which is at least clear in its evaluation of the state of the world from a historical viewpoint.

All the above approaches—and we use the term broadly—have their variants, sub-variants and differing interpretations. Many contradict each other, and even themselves, as well as overlap with each other. Picture to yourself the heaving mass of Venn diagrams mentioned in Chapter 1, each section saying something sensible, but also disputable. None is perfect: for example, are there not states that have *not* passed through the same stages as other states? Most books on modern Greece say that Greece passed into the Industrial Revolution far later than Britain; but was there ever an Industrial Revolution in Greece? Was it not more a case of importing foreign manufacturing methods, rather than going through what Britain went through? And was not Britain's power based on its empire, while modern Greece had no empire?

Let us refer back to Chapter 1, and the seminar that took place to try and resolve the questions raised by international relations theory, part of the conclusions of which read: 'Historically, international relations as a discipline has come to view dialogue and synthesis as incompatible objectives. [...] As a community of scholars, however, we are equally compelled to compete, - an important reason why we prefer debate over dialogue and pluralism over synthesis'.[8] This was really an honest, if subtle, admission that a single all-embracing theory of relations between states is a chimera. The uncomfortable question even arises as to whether international relations is a discipline or a subject that sucks in other ones, unlike history, which needs to understand other fields, while not depending on them per se. There are so many books on international relations, and so many interpretations, as to detract from intellectual stability. One is permitted to wonder whether it is a subject or a discipline[9] and to what extent it can be considered to be a science. Many subjects have been labelled as sciences, simply to position them as academically respectable. A certain, if not precise, parallel can be drawn with public relations, the allegedly academic study of which began at New York University, in 1923. In the attempt to elevate it from being a government and business propagandistic activity to a serious subject, communications theory was 'lifted' from other disciplines, just as happened with the study of international relations. The result was that a fair number of practitioners and theorists preferred the word 'communications' to 'relations'. Communications theory, which itself had drawn on various scientific theories, was used by many teachers of public relations: the five main communications perspectives were the mechanistic, pragmatic, psychological, interactionist and dramatist. Just as public relations is considered by many practitioners to be public communications, so could the subject of international relations end up being described as 'international communications'. Such are the vagaries of trying to create academically respectable theories out of what were originally intended to be simple, or at least comprehensible, activities. We can now better understand what Lin Yutang wrote (see above) about Man's obsession with words and definitions.

The confusion does not end here: one expert writes that there are three contending *approaches* to the field of international relations: realism, pluralism and structuralism.[10] On the other hand, the *Penguin Dictionary of International Relations* states that with the [alleged] end of the Cold War), there are four competing *paradigms*: neorealism, neoliberalism, critical theory and post-modernism,[11] while the renowned Stephen Walt writes of three *traditions*: realism, liberalism and radicalism. Then, seemingly self-confusingly, he adds a diagram (model?), listing realism and liberalism, but adding constructivism.[12] Is the reader intended to think that a paradigm is a tradition, and radicalism is constructivism?

Attempt to Clarify

One international historian tries to hack through the semantic Gordian Knot, referring to three schools, the realist, behaviouralist and structuralist, but then refers to them as paradigms. He nevertheless sensibly states that they all overlap, and that it is not therefore easy to choose, since one needs to be acquainted with a host of disciplines such as history, politics, sociology, economics, law, psychology, anthropology and philosophy, 'to name but a few'.[13] Here we see the beginning of some common sense. But then we turn to some recent ideas: it seems that the attempt to clarify is being bedevilled by further contradictions, in that the study of international relations appears, according to an expert, to have moved from the emphasis placed on biology by social Darwinism (appreciated by many political realists and fans of geopolitics) to physics, and recently back to biology.[14] The expert explains this by arguing that Francis Fukuyama (see above), having realised that his contention that the 'end of history' had been reached with Western liberal democracy's victory over fascism, absolutism and communism was mistaken, changed his tune, emphasising 'masculine values rooted in biology', going on to say that 'female chimps have relationships', while (see Chapter 1) 'male chimps practice *Realpolitik*'.[15] Fukuyama is quoted as adding that because (he claims) the line from chimp to modern man is continuous, this has significant consequences for international politics.[16]

Conclusions

Although we have pointed to the confusion reigning in international relations theory, and suggested reasons for this, it is important to understand that we are not trying to debunk all theory, let alone the study of relations between states, but advocating a simpler, more reliable and less controversial method of understanding these relations, that transcends brain-suffocating ideologies. Nonetheless, were it not for the very efforts in understanding the theories that we have considered, we would have some difficulty in explaining geohistory in Chapter 6, since it is the very fact that matters need clarification that in turn will lead us to geohistory.

Completely clarifying international relations theory has never proven possible, although a certain amount of distilling can be done. The essential problem is the floppy thinking and obsession with definition which can lead to confusion: the theories, ideas, paradigms, schools, traditions, perspectives, approaches, most with their divisions and sub-divisions, many being interpreted and re-interpreted owing to often unforeseeable events, all enrich thinking about international relations, or international politics (depending on one's viewpoint), but do not clarify. Perhaps this explains why political realism attracts geopoliticians: there are less Procrustean models and cherry-picking to fit the model, and less 'interference' from other academic areas. But claims by some political realists that their approach is based on human behaviour ring false, since they are thinking mainly about *mass* human behaviour, rather than analysing behaviour emanating from the human nature so vital to Guicciardini who, for example, writes: 'You may count more safely on one who has need of you, or who for the time has the same ends to serve, than on one whom you have benefitted, for, as a rule, men are ungrateful. If you would not be deceived, make your calculations on this footing'.[17] Another Guicciardini gem is: 'Frank sincerity pleases all men, and is a noble quality, though sometimes hurtful to him who practises it. Simulation, on the other hand, is useful; nay, from the perverse nature of men is often necessary, odious and unseemly though it be'.[18] At the bottom lies human nature and its concomitant characteristics/traits, which lead to how people behave.

However, sceptical one might be about this or that theory, they can serve as brain stimulants, but also addle thinking, if one sinks too deep into the semantic quagmire. Interestingly, an expert begins to approach some of what we shall be arguing in connexion with human behaviour, by drawing on Socrates, and inventing a 'new'[19] theory (he then calls it a 'paradigm') based on fear, interest and honour. But he then slightly confuses the issue by mentioning spirit, appetite and reason as 'fundamental drives'.[20] Yet many would dispute this, since spirit is surely something in its own right, and not a 'drive'.

Every theory has something to contribute, but none is sufficient to enable complete detached understanding of the state of relations between

Fig. 3.2 The scramble for IR, by the artist David Mallinson

states and therefore all-encompassing solutions. Perhaps they are reflection of the state of the world, in that they are themselves part of history. If you now feel slightly confused, then I have achieved my aim, thus far.

All the above being said and offered for your consideration, let us now turn to geopolitics (Fig. 3.2).

Notes

1. Published as an epigraph for Chapter 1, on page 5 of my book Behind the Words: The FCO, Hegemonolingualism and the End of Britain's Freedom, Cambridge Scholars Publishing, 2014, 2016. I took the quote from a paper by Dionisis Menzeniotis, 'Demystifying Knowledge Society and Its Alleged 'Education', *Cosmothemata*, vol. 2, no. 2, New York College, Athens, 2005, which in turn took the quote from Eliot, T.S., *The Rock*, Faber and Faber, London, 1934.
2. Yutang, Lin, *The Importance of Living*, William Heinemann Ltd., London, 1976, p. 404.

3. Rengger, Nicholas, 'Political Theory and International Relations: Promised Land or Exit from Eden?' *International Affairs*, vol. 76, no. 4, Blackwell, Oxford, October 2000, pp. 755–770, in Mallinson, William, *Cyprus, Diplomatic History and the Clash of Theory in International Relations*, I.B. Tauris, London and New York, 2010, p. 18.
4. *Daily Telegraph*, 25 March 1992, 'Obituary', in Mallinson, Bill, *Public Lies and Private Truths: An Anatomy of Public Relations*, Cassell, London and New York, 1996, and Leader Books, Athens, 2000, p. 66.
5. Strange, Susan, 'States, Firms and Diplomacy', *International Affairs*, vol. 68, no. 1, January 1992, Royal Institute of International Affairs, p. 15.
6. Evans, Graham and Newnham, Geoffrey, *The Penguin Dictionary of International Relations*, Penguin, London etc., 1998, p. 148.
7. Strauss, Leo and Cropsey, Joseph (eds.), *History of Political Philosophy*, University of Chicago, 1987 (first published in 1963).
8. Hellman, Gunther (ed.), 'Are Dialogue and Synthesis Possible in International Relations?' *International Studies Review*, Blackwell, Malden (USA), and Oxford, 2003.
9. Berridge, G.R., *International Politics*, Pearson Education, Harlow, 2002, p. 2.
10. Ibid.
11. Evans, Graham and Newnham, Geoffrey, *The Penguin Dictionary of International Relations*, Penguin, London etc., 1998, p. 417.
12. Walt, Stephen, 'International Relations: One World, Many Theories', *Foreign Policy*, Washington, Spring 1998, pp. 30 and 38.
13. Sked, Alan, 'The Study of International Relations: A Historian's View', Dyer, Hugh C. and Mangasarian, Leon (eds.), *The Study of International Relations*, Macmillan, Basingstoke and London, 1989, p. 91.
14. Bell, Duncan, 'Beware of False Prophets: Biology, Human Nature and the Future of International Relations Theory', *International Affairs*, Vol. 82, No. 3, Chatham House, London, May, 2006.
15. Whether or not Fukuyama understands the difference between political realism/power politics and *realpolitik* must remain a moot point.
16. Op. cit., Bell, Duncan, p. 501. Fukuyama's critics might well suggest that Fukuyama sees himself as the missing link.
17. Op. cit., Guicciardini, *Ricordi*, 264, pp. 112–113.
18. Ibid., 104, p. 47.
19. 'New', because little is really new: theorists have been re-inventing the wheel for millennia. Nevertheless, ancient experts still have enormous influence.
20. Lebow, Richard Ned, 'Fear, Interest and Honour: Outlines of a Theory of International Relations', in op. cit., *International Affairs*, vol. 82, no. 3, pp. 431–448.

Bibliography

Bell, Duncan, 'Beware of False Prophets: Biology, Human Nature and the Future of International Relations Theory', *International Affairs*, Vol. 82, No. 3, Chatham House, London, May, 2006.

Berridge, G. R., *International Politics* , Pearson Education, Harlow, 2002.

Evans, Graham and Newnham, Geoffrey, *The Penguin Dictionary of International Relations*, Penguin, London etc., 1998.

Guicciardini, Francesco, *Counsels and Reflections*, translated from the Italian (*Ricordi Politici e Civili*) by Ninian Hill Thomson, M.A., Kegan Paul, Trench Trübner & Co., Ltd., London, 1890.

Hellman, Gunther (ed.), 'Are Dialogue and Synthesis Possible in International Relations?' *International Studies Review*, Blackwell, Malden (USA), and Oxford, 2003.

Mallinson, Bill, *Public Lies and Private Truths: An Anatomy of Public Relations*, Cassell, London and New York, 1996, and Leader Books, Athens, 2000.

Mallinson, William, *Cyprus, Diplomatic History and the Clash of Theory in International Relations*, I.B. Tauris, London and New York, 2010.

Mallinson, William, *Behind the Words: The FCO, Hegemonolingualism and the End of Britain's Freedom*, Cambridge Scholars Publishing, Newcastle upon Tyne, 2014, 2016.

Sked, Alan, 'The Study of International Relations: A Historian's View', Dyer, Hugh C. and Mangasarian, Leon (eds.), *The Study of International Relations*, Macmillan, Basingstoke and London, 1989.

Strange, Susan, 'States, Firms and Diplomacy', *International Affairs*, vol. 68, no. 1, January 1992, Royal Institute of International Affairs.

Strauss, Leo and Cropsey, Joseph (eds.), *History of Political Philosophy*, University of Chicago, 1987 (first published in 1963).

Walt, Stephen, 'International Relations: One World, Many Theories', *Foreign Policy*, Washington, Spring 1998.

Yutang, Lin, *The Importance of Living*, William Heinemann Ltd., London, 1976.

CHAPTER 4

Geopolitics and the Politicisation of Geography

Abstract This chapter traces the origin of the term geopolitics as an imperial tool, how it went out of fashion and was then re-introduced. It considers how geography has been politicised and points out that geopolitics is a mainstay of political realism/power politics. The result is that it tends to sweep the human factor under the carpet, since it is concerned with the acquiring of resources, such as oil, which has included the drawing up of 'business borders' according to the interests of large powers, rather than natural borders. The Sykes-Picot agreement is used as an example.

Keywords Geography · Mackinder · Haushofer · Kissinger · Greece · Russia · Imperial

> Geographical diversity versus geopolitical uniformity

INTRODUCTION

The term 'geopolitics' is used willy-nilly these days, and increasingly so, mainly by international relations academics, think-tankers, politicians and foreign affairs officials, in the belief that the term adds academic respectability to what they are propounding. Sometimes, they confuse the

© The Author(s), under exclusive license to Springer Nature
Switzerland AG 2021
W. Mallinson, *Guicciardini, Geopolitics and Geohistory*,
Palgrave Studies in International Relations,
https://doi.org/10.1007/978-3-030-76537-8_4

word with 'geostrategy'.[1] More than sometimes, they even tend to use it to explain and justify military attacks, whether legal or not. Certainly, the term has entered the hegemonolinguistic terminology of globalisation, along with such simplistic terms as 'shared values', 'shoulder to shoulder', 'going forward', 'forces of good'[2] and the like. Some speakers can be likened to auto-brainwashed humans who no longer properly understand what they are saying: in Orwellian terms, the right noises come out of the larynx, but the speaker is in a reduced state of consciousness, which is of course favourable to political conformity.[3] According to Agatha Christie, a wise old Frenchman once said: 'Speech is an invention of Man to prevent him from thinking'.[4] Many of those using the term 'geopolitics' have not studied its origins, let alone its meaning and implications. Once some of them begin to try and understand it, they are attracted by world maps, simply because looking at maps is easier and less painstaking than reading words. As such, they run the danger of being trapped, albeit unknowingly, in a simplistic view of the world, a world where only the woods matter, while the trees become boring irrelevancies, let alone the branches, twigs, buds, flowers, nuts and leaves. Guicciardini makes the point well: 'Small and almost imperceptible beginnings are often the occasion of great disasters or of great prosperity. The highest prudence therefore lies in noting and weighing well all circumstances, even the most trifling'.[5]

Geopolitics has—insidiously for many—been affecting the lives we lead to an increasing extent, aided by the so-called phenomenon of globalisation. Let us begin to define the term.

Defining Geopolitics

According to *The Penguin Dictionary of International Relations*, geopolitics is 'a method of foreign policy analysis which seeks to understand, explain and predict international political behaviour primarily in terms of geographical variables, such as location, size, climate, topography, demography, natural resources and technological development and potential. Political identity and action are thus seen to be more (more or less) determined by geography'.[6] That may sound fine as far as it goes, although it does not mention behaviour *within* nations. Nor is space given to the human characteristics that give rise to political behaviour. More succinctly, the *Concise Oxford Dictionary* defines it thus: 'the politics of a country as determined by its geographical features; the study of this'.[7] One academic of geopolitics views it as 'an X-ray of reality and thus the study of the distribution of power internationally, the four kinds of power being military, economic, political and cultural/informational'. 'This', he says, 'implies the existence of geostrategy' or, as he puts it, 'political intervention to transform or intensify the results of geopolitical analysis'.[8] Again there is no mention of human characteristics, unsurprising, perhaps, given his academic qualifications in rural engineering and economic geography. Morality and people rarely figure in geopolitics or, indeed, in its theoretical friend political realism. In direct contrast to the above, geohistory (see Chapter 6) focuses on understanding individual and corporate characteristics and behaviour. Indeed, geopolitics, unlike neutral and dispassionate geohistory, can restrict free analysis and evaluation, constrained as it is by its obsession with the control of resources, which is one of the causes of war. Here, geohistory clashes with the likes of Hegel, who appeared to believe that war brought progress.[9] Like several German philosophers, Heraclitus' famous but over-used saying 'strife is justice' seems to have been accompanied by an excess of logic. The contention that war can bring progress seems arbitrary, simplistic and misguided: it may be true that land is sometimes burnt for agricultural reasons, to improve the next crop; but people are hardly to be equated with crops. In a materialistic sense, destruction of a large amount of Europe's infrastructure in the last world war may well have led to faster trains, while in Britain, with less damage, the trains remained slower. But slower trains can hardly be taken as an example of lack of progress. To put the point more strongly, does owning an I-phone imply progress? Not if one juxtaposes it with giving knives and forks to cannibals.

The point here is that advanced technology cannot have any serious effect on the basic human characteristics, other than inducing humans to move faster, with all the concomitant adverse effects, such as lack of space to properly reflect on one's actions.

To return to our defining of geopolitics, let us consider the words of the US Air Force, since they represent 'geopolitical thinking' *par excellence*: American airmen are 'engaged defending US interests around the globe, supporting Combatant Commander requirements in response to growing challenges from Russia, China, North Korea and Iran [...] The United States Air Force continues to be the world's finest Air Force across the spectrum of conflict, but our potential adversaries employ increasingly sophisticated, capable, and lethal systems. The Air Force must modernise to deter, deny, and decisively defeat any actor that threatens the homeland and our national interests. [...] Our sister services and allies expect the Air Force to provide critical warfighting and enabling capabilities. We remain focused on delivering Global Vigilance, Reach and Power, through our core missions of Air Superiority, Space Superiority, Global Strike, Rapid Global Mobility, Intelligence, Surveillance and Reconnaissance and Command and Control. We look forward to working closely with the committee to ensure the ability to deliver combat air power for America when and where we are needed'.[10]

The above represents what many would consider to be 'imperialistic geopolitics', or what many now refer to as 'meta-imperial', since to admit that imperialism still abounds in our 'advanced' world is not politically correct. It is clear that the US armed forces still consider that America is the world's only superpower, and that they believe that US interests are worldwide. If interests are to be measured by having over one thousand military bases worldwide (many of them taken over from former British colonies), then the US does indeed have worldwide interests, but mainly of a military nature. Let us now introduce more precision to what geopolitics is, by looking briefly at the history of geography; how the term 'geopolitics' came to be, along with its early proponents; its temporary unpopularity; and its resuscitation. Let us begin with the exploitation of geography.

POLITICISATION OF GEOGRAPHY

In Ancient Greece, 'geography' (a Greek word, meaning 'earth-writing') was fairly unpolemical, given that it dealt mainly with the physical characteristics of our planet. Several ancient Greeks are credited with works on geography, including even Homer. As mapping became increasingly sophisticated with the circumnavigation of the world, so the study of geography was taken more seriously as an academic subject, being taught at European universities by the eighteenth century. The German van Humboldt gave a big impetus to the subject, with his *Kosmos: A Sketch of a Physical Description of the Universe*, published in 1845. Although the physical description of peoples was a necessary part of geography—human geography—the subject was still fairly unsullied by political ideology. In Britain, the first full chair for geography was not established until 1917, although the Royal Geographical Society had been founded in 1830, when the term 'geopolitics' was still unknown. So how did the term 'geopolitics' come about?

The Industrial Revolution, the economic growth mentality and new technologies led to an intensification in colonising, particularly the 'scramble for Africa'. Economic rivalry and 'resource-hunting' were major causes of the Great War. Although two world wars had already taken place (the Seven Years' War and the Napoleonic War), the term 'geopolitics'—as opposed to greedy imperial thinking—had not yet entered the vocabulary. An American naval officer, Alfred Mahan (1840–1914), although he did not specifically use the term, is considered to be one of the earliest exponents of the modern geopolitical mentality. He emphasised sea power as the best method of projecting a country's power worldwide (emulating Britain), thus introducing a naval arms race.[11] Like Britain, he also considered it necessary to resist Russia, thus continuing the former's preoccupation with that country, when William Pitt the Younger had denounced Russia in 1791 for wishing to dismember Anatolia.[12] The Cold War began earlier than most people have been led to think.

Mahan influenced a German geographer and zoologist, Friedrich Ratzel (1844–1904), who also believed in naval power, but concentrated his writings more on land: ominously, this follower of Darwin's theories was the first person to coin the term *'Lebensraum'* ('living space'), in an essay on 'biogeopolitik'. This term led to the use of the term 'geopolitik': the Swede Rudolf Kjellen (1864–1922), influenced by Ratzel, used the term. By now, the German approach laid particular emphasis on the state being an organic entity, thus implying that strong and growing states could break down borders in the quest to grow. War was thus on the backstage agenda.

To add to the imperialist elements of geopolitics, and to lend an Anglo-Saxon flavour to Mahan's work, the Briton Halford Mackinder (1861–1947) threw his hat into the ring. This geographer certainly politicised geography, mainly through his near obsession with Russia. Although he himself did not use the term geopolitics in his famous essay 'The Geographical Pivot of History',[13] he clearly injected British imperial thinking into his ideas. He was obsessed with German and Russian power and feared an alliance between those two countries. For him, Russia constituted the pivot area of the 'world island' of Eurasia. He referred to the importance of teaching the British masses, who were of 'limited intelligence', to think imperially.[14] The sharp end of his views can be summarised in the following: 'The oversetting of the balance of power in favour of the pivot state, resulting in its expansion over the marginal lands of Euro-Asia, would permit the use of vast continental resources for fleet-building, and the empire of the world would then be in sight. This might happen if Germany were to ally herself with Russia'.[15] 'Who rules East Europe commands the Heartland; who rules the Heartland commands the World-Island; who rules the World-Island commands the World'.[16]

Although Mackinder's emphasis on land power was not adhered to early on, since naval power was considered to be of a higher priority, his ideas became increasingly influential, particularly when allied to those such as Ratzel. The idea of the *Drang nach Osten* of the Middle Ages was back with a vengeance: the superior German race, with its natural attachment to the soil, would thrust eastwards, while the superior Anglo-Saxons would teach the world true civilisation with their superior naval power. The clash between British and German economic interests that was a chief cause of the Great War had as part of its backcloth the British fear of a German-Russian alliance, especially after the Treaty of Brest-Litovsk in early 1918, when Germany and Russia made peace. In line with Guicciardini's thinking, matters are the same today, with the US and Britain doing their utmost to undermine German-Russian co-operation, of which the supply of Russian gas to Germany is but one aspect. Let us now look at some of the less savoury aspects of the imperial and racial underpinnings of the modern origins of geopolitics.

Supremacy

One does not need to read Kipling and others to suspect that the English establishment felt somewhat superior to many foreigners, just as the German establishment tended to. Perhaps, in a perverse fashion, the nationalism that grew out of the French Revolution had subtly affected even some of the phlegmatic English, notwithstanding their having been instrumental in Napoleon's defeat. For example, Sir Francis Younghusband (famous for having led the invasion of Tibet in 1904) wrote: 'Our superiority over them [Indians] is not due to mere sharpness of intellect, but to the higher moral nature to which we have attained in the development of the human race'.[17] Not to be outdone, a Liberal Member of Parliament, Sir Charles Dilke, considered America as the agent of Anglo-Saxon domination, predicting a great racial conflict from which 'Saxendom would rise triumphant' with China, Japan, Africa and South America soon falling to the all-conquering Anglo-Saxon, and Italy, Spain, France and Russia 'becoming pygmies by the side of such people'.[18]

Of particular interest is the fact that Dilke did not mention Germany. He could hardly do so since the English were almost exclusively descended (at least then) from the tribes which invaded Southern Britain after the Romans left, destroying the prevailing Romano-Celtic culture. Thus, at least to people of Dilke's ilk, England and Germany were closely connected in terms of superiority. Here lies the paradox, contradiction, even: this whole way of thinking was to pit the English against their German blood brothers into two of the most devastating wars known to Mankind. But before focusing on the German brand of geopolitics, let us develop our English imperial theme, so dear to Mackinder.

We see the origins of the emotional side of the 'special relationship' between Britain and America, the latter being run by an Anglo-Saxon élite or, in more familiar modern terminology, White Anglo-Saxon Protestants (WASPs). While the American establishment had their indigenous 'red vermin' and imported Negroes as whipping boys, the British had their disdain for those south of Calais. Those readers of this book who happen to have attended English Prep Schools up to at least the late Seventies may well remember not only simplistic history books such as *Little Arthur's History of England* or *Our Island Story*, but fellow schoolboys using such terms as 'Philistine', 'Jew', 'yid', 'gypo', 'frog', 'wog', 'dago', 'hun', 'slit-eye' and the like. Winston Churchill himself wrote about the 'schemes of the International Jew', referring to a 'sinister confederacy', and describing them as a 'world-wide conspiracy for the overthrow of civilisation and for the reconstitution of society'.[19] It is not of course only the English who were somewhat supercilious vis-à-vis foreigners: the French were to have their 'Croix de Feu' to compete with Mosley's Blackshirts, while the American Henry Ford's book *The International Jew* is too well known to merit further elaboration. We shall see later how these racial/imperialistic factors (that, oddly, were spawned by the Enlightenment) are still with us today, albeit in different colours, with the Arabs, as well as the Jews, being targeted, and how the likes of George Bush Junior, Donald Rumsfeld, Paul Wolfowitz, Madeleine Albright, Condoleezza Rice and Richard Cheney stoked the fire. But let us now turn to Germany, that other member of Saxendom.

SURFEIT OF LOGIC

As we have already intimated—and shall expand on in Chapter 6—geohistory is predicated on human characteristics and the behaviour emanating from them. The tactile Italians Guicciardini and Vico[20] are, as we shall see later, closer to our views on relations between states than are some of the most well-known German philosophers, who appear to lay inordinate emphasis on German racial superiority and, in particular, power, the latter appealing to political realists. Nietzsche's thinking hinges on the idea of the *Übermensch* (superior being), much exploited by the Nazis. Hegel's view of history, approached in a coldly logical and intensely rational manner, promotes the idea of divine German perfection. Like some other German philosophers, he latched on to some of the pre-Socratic philosophers, Heraclitus in particular, who had written that 'strife is justice'. Interpreting rather literally, Hegel tended to glorify war. Marx, who was keen on Democritus, and therefore believed in materialism, replaced God and religion with society and economics, the fight being for the control of the means of production. We mention these political thinkers because, unlike Guicciardini, they politicised history, just as Ratzel et al. politicised geography. The ideas of these 'geographical and historical' thinkers were to influence those interested in power, to the detriment of peace, culminating in the Great War. Thus we turn to the next war and Haushofer, as the last of our early geopoliticians, and to the Nazi connexion.

Haushofer

Karl Haushofer[21] believed in Mackinder's heartland theory,[22] and, perhaps forewarned by the latter's ideas, therefore argued for an alliance between Germany and Russia. He was impressed by Japanese expansionism when a German army officer in that country. Promoted to major-general by the end of the Great War, he devoted himself to Germany's regeneration, studying political geography, becoming a professor, and directing the Institute of Geopolitics at Munich University. His closeness to Hitler's deputy, Rudolf Hess, a former student of his, meant that his influence in military circles was enormous, and he was instrumental in forging Japan's alliance with Germany. Above all, his ideas were used to justify Germany's territorial expansion. It is here that we see the merging of Ratzel's, Kjellen's and Mackinder's ideas into a potent translation of geopolitics into geostrategy, that was to contribute to the Fourth World War.[23] Given the strong association between Nazi ideology and geopolitics, the latter was discredited for a while. Indeed, British and American academic circles, claiming—perhaps with a hint of hypocrisy—that Haushofer and the Institute of Geopolitics were using geography for power-political purposes, preferred the term 'political geography'. But this was more a matter of semantic pirouetting. For a time, at any rate, the term 'geopolitics' went into hibernation.

THE RETURN OF GEOPOLITICS

As often in US academic life, it was immigrants, believing in the necessity of American power, who built on the study of geopolitics after the war. Nicholas Spykman, an émigré from the Netherlands, who taught at Yale University, was an early pioneer of the continuation of geopolitical ideas, basing most of his thinking on Mahan's and Mackinder's ideas, hardly original, in that he was re-inventing the wheel, as Guicciardini, in particular, would understand. He slightly adapted Mackinder's definitions, for example by re-naming Mackinder's 'inner or marginal crescent' as 'rimland'. To the unity of sea and land, he also added the air. He argued strongly that the balance of power in Eurasia affected America, and that the latter therefore needed influence in Europe. Most significantly, he was concurrently one of the most influential founders of the realist/power politics school. Had he not died in 1943, he would have had a yet greater impact than he did, but nevertheless made his mark with the publication of *The Geography of the Peace*[24] in the year after his death. Like virtually all geopolitical people, he was obsessed with Russia and can thus be viewed as an early Cold War warrior.

It was political realists such as Zbigniew Brzezinski[25] and Henry Kissinger who took over the anti-Soviet/Russian Cold War baton. The former was unashamedly dedicated to containing the USSR, even advocating in 1986 the possibility of a nuclear strike on the USSR against 'its imperial great Russian component',[26] thereby introducing an ethnic factor into geopolitics to the extent of transmogrifying parts of geostrategy into 'ethnopolitics'. Kissinger, with his alleged policy of détente, was subtler. Both academics served, inter alia, as National Security Advisers, Brzezinski taking over from Kissinger in 1977. Well before their political heyday, the concept of geopolitics had become inextricably intertwined with political realism/power politics. After all, the more emphasis one lays on the use and projection of power in theorising about or practicing international politics, the more attractive the term becomes to those who wish to use force. In this sense, the phrase 'power projection' is often simply a euphemism for force and war.

As the Cold War progressed, the geopolitical mentality again came to the fore, coming into its own with the fall of the Berlin Wall in 1989. Paradoxically, it was 'the arch-priest of the rational use of power',[27] Kissinger (see above), a German Jewish immigrant of all people, whom one would have assumed to dislike Haushofer's Nazi-connected ideas, who 'almost single-handedly helped to revive the term "geopolitics" in the 1970s, by using it as a synonym for the superpower game of balance-of-power politics'.[28] One can indeed argue that Kissinger, realising how controversial the term 'geopolitics' was, simply disguised his extreme realist agenda in the clothes of the 'balance of power', a balance of power that of course had many sides, one being that it could provide the US with a blank cheque to pursue its own agenda. But what is the elusive 'balance of power'? Let us quote Henry Kissinger's comments: 'Theorists of the balance of power often leave the impression that it is the natural form of international relations. In fact, balance-of-power systems have existed only rarely in human history. The Western Hemisphere has never known one, nor has the territory of contemporary China since the end of the period of the warring states, over 2,000 years ago. For the greatest part of humanity and the longest periods of history, empire has been the typical mode of government. Empires have no interest in operating within an international system; they aspire to *be* the international system. That is how the United States has conducted its foreign policy in the Americas, and China throughout most of its history in Asia'.[29] Having established that empires were the order of the day, and that America is not interested in the balance of power, he does then go on to acknowledge that Ancient Greece and Renaissance Italy were the only examples of functioning balance-of-power systems.[30] But he does not offer us a definition of balance of power. In this connexion, it was Guicciardini who seriously considered the concept, believing, as we have seen, in balancing potentially hostile forces. More perspicaciously than the vaguer Kissinger, Martin Wight wrote: 'Compared with the pattern if power, the notion of the balance of power is notoriously full of confusions, so that it is impossible to make any statement about the "law" or principle of the balance of power that will command general acceptance'.[31]

Geohistory does not need to attempt a definition of the balance of power, but merely to record and understand that it is a product of individual and corporate ways of interpreting and conducting relations between states. In Kissinger's case, a geohistorian would likely come to the conclusion that he used the idea to justify geopolitics, and the US's never having participated in a balance-of-power system. One could argue here that the Cold War developed by force of circumstance into a *modus vivendi*, that is now being shaken. A geohistorian might simply conclude that a multipolar system is developing.

A. J. P. Taylor's view is that Metternich did not invent the balance of power, nor do much to develop it, and that the great powers of Europe existed without his assistance. 'Metternich did not invent the Balance of Power, nor do much to develop it. The great powers of Europe existed without his assistance; [...] His only answer to either liberalism or radicalism was, in fact, repression'.[32]

If the idea of the balance of power, inter alia, has been exploited as a geopolitical idea, at least in the Atlantic/Western world, the term geopolitics, and its study, came late to Russia.

THE WORLD ISLAND HITS BACK

Although a geopolitician can argue that Russia's behaviour since its inception has been geopolitical, in the sense that it has become the 'world island' through territorial expansion, and gaining access to the Mediterranean, and the creation of buffer states to protect its borders, geopolitics per se was not formally studied in name until fairly recently. Although Petr Nikoloyevitch (1895–1968), for example, is known for his Eurasian Movement, and the idea of a strong Russia, independent of Europe and Asia, he was not associated with the term 'geopolitics' until recently, as with an earlier thinker, Nikolai Danilevsky (1822–1885), who was one of the main proponents of Pan-Slavism. It was only after the break-up of the Soviet Union that the study of geopolitics in name came into its own. According to one Russian academic, Russian geopolitics, while having emerged as a vocation, has yet to turn into a fully-fledged academic discipline, lacking coherent and scientifically testable theoretical propositions (the same can be said of geopolitics in the West).[33]

At any event, following the fall of the Berlin Wall and the subsequent break-up of the Soviet Union, Russia's leading geopolitician, Alexandr Dugin (also a political analyst and philosopher), interested in Haushofer's ideas, introduced his version of geopolitics, going rather further than Mackinder et al., by dividing the world into four major regions: Asia-Pacific, dominated by Japan; Euro-Africa, dominated by the EU; Anglo-Saxon, including Great Britain and Australia; and Russia-Eurasia, dominated by Russia, and including the Middle East and Central

Asia. He advocated the erosion of American power, through supporting isolationist groups in America, and supporting anti-American tendencies in Latin America (here, Venezuela springs to mind). To quote from his book: 'Every geopolitical level of the US should be involved simultaneously, similar to the anti-Eurasianism of the Atlanticists, who have "sponsored" the disintegration of the strategic bloc (Warsaw Pact), governmental unity (USSR), and furthered ethno-territorial problems under the guise of regionalism [...] The Heartland will force the Sea Power to pay in the same coin. This is basic symmetrical politics'.[34]

Dugin also advocates, inter alia, a Moscow-Berlin axis, cutting Britain off from Europe, the annexation of the Ukraine, the dismemberment of Georgia, and a Moscow-Tehran axis, all of which must have Mackinder spinning in his grave. Much of what he advocates has come true, if only partially.

This was of course a reaction to NATO's reneging on a 'gentleman's agreement' not to expand to Russia's borders; to Western support for various pro-Western NGOs in Russia; the illegal bombing of Serbia; and the first Gulf War. As such it can be justified from a Russian viewpoint.

CRITIQUE

It was a combination of imperialist ambition and a geopolitical mentality that led to the (mis)drawing of many of the world's current borders. An obvious example is the secret Sykes-Picot agreement of 1916 (see next chapter), which led to all manner of future tensions and wars in the Middle East, which continue to this day. Needless to say, oil interests came to the forefront, and the Gulf States of today can be seen as Sykes' and Picot's delinquent children, just as the mistimed and clumsily implemented creation of the state of Israel can. Another example is the partition of India, which led to the killings of up to a million people, and mass migration, on the part of Hindus, Sikhs and Moslems. Here, we need to qualify: the partition cannot be solely attributed to a British imperial mentality: Stafford Cripps worked hard at keeping India together, and Lord Mountbatten was also instructed to keep the country together. But in the face of Moslem pressure, led by the likes of Ali Jinnah, even Gandhi succumbed to partition. Britain also wished to get out as soon as practicable. Today, the Kashmir problem can nevertheless be seen as the sting in the tail of a geopolitical mentality, in the sense that Britain took a geopolitical decision.

It is at any event hardly surprising that some of the most respected experts in international relations are highly critical of geopolitics. Christopher Hill, for example, describes it as 'a primitive form of International Relations theory',[35] while Ó Tuathail reduces it to the level of being 'about contested claims to knowledge'.[36] To obtain some of the critical flavour, let us quote Hill at more length: 'The military balance and the economic league tables are intimately connected to a society's physical patrimony. In the first half of the twentieth century some influential academic work on geopolitics, which we may recognise as a primitive form of International Relations theory, produced largely[37] by geographers, suggested that this matrix had a decisive effect on a state's foreign policy, and indeed on the global balance of power. Various factors were identified at different phases of this intellectual fashion; when taken up by policy-makers they became semi-fulfilling prophesies, ultimately with disastrous results. All revealed the obsession of the times with a neo-Darwinian view of international relations as struggle and survival, which reached its nadir in fascism'.[38]

Alfred Mahan, as we have seen, was the first to seriously influence policy-formulation, by emphasising the importance of sea power: President Theodore Roosevelt decided to build up the navy and ensure US control of the new Panama Canal (in the Hay-Bunau-Varilla Treaty of 1903). But unlike Mahan, Mackinder and Haushofer believed that power was moving to those controlling great land masses, and in particular the 'heartland' of the 'world-island' of Eurasia. This provided Hitler with some of the ideas which he needed for the policies of *Lebensraum* and European domination. The horrors of the war then discredited overtly geopolitical theories, but this did not prevent ideas like the 'iron curtain', 'containment' and the 'domino theory' perpetuating the belief that foreign policy had to 'follow strategic imperatives deriving from the territorial distribution of power across the earth's surface'.[39]

Having put the term geopolitics into a chronological context, let us now consider where it is today, and why we consider it to be inadequate academically, and indeed in terms of ensuring stability in our world.

Now Is then

While Hill is succinct and incisive in his description of geopolitics above, he appears to be optimistic when he goes on to write that geopolitics in the old sense (until the end of the Cold War) will soon be a mere curiosity.

He is perhaps slightly jumping the gun here, if we take Guicciardini's advice to heart: 'The affairs of this world are so shifting and depend on so many accidents, that it is hard to form any judgment concerning the future; nay, we see from experience that the forecasts even of the wise almost always turn out false'.[40] Hill's book was published just before the US-led attacks on Iraq and Libya, and the attempt to attack Syria, the latter thwarted only by incisive action by Russia.

Unfortunately for many, geopolitics still seems to be all the rage. Nothing has really seriously modified since the alleged end of the Cold War: indeed, there is scant evidence that it has ended, unless one considers the fall of the Berlin Wall and chaotic Yeltsin years as a temporary lull, bearing in mind, nevertheless, that the Cold War was/is more about economic interests than ideology, the latter being a convenient excuse to feed to the masses.

As for Syria, in the world limelight as this is being written, John F. Kennedy's nephew and namesake has said that the US decided to remove President Assad because he had refused to back a Qatari gas pipeline project.[41] The pipeline would have originated in Qatar, crossed Syria (sucking in its offshore reserves), and continued through Turkey to the EU, thereby competing directly with Russia's Gazprom. Thus the West's attempt to attack Syria was simply a continuation of politics by other means (to coin a phrase from von Clausewitz) or, more fashionably put, an attempt to apply geostrategy. Whether or not one agrees with Kennedy, the putative Qatari pipeline was an important factor.

Shades of the above-mentioned Sykes-Picot agreement return here, to remind us that certain Arab states were created because of oil interests. Saudi Arabia and the Gulf States come to mind. The fact that the close links of these countries to the West can be explained geopolitically (thanks to oil or, as I call it, black blood) demonstrates that geopolitics today has little to do with people or morality, but more with the interests of large corporations and the governments that support them in the name of national interests. People become geostrategic fodder. Before concluding this chapter, let us remind ourselves of Guicciardini's maxim that things have always been the same, by describing and considering some aspects of Anglo-Greek relations.

Britain's well-known keenness to keep Russia, the Soviet Union, and now again just Russia, away from the Eastern Mediterranean is a well-established fact. Since the end of the last world war, the same policy has returned, albeit in the new colours of America, with the UK in attendance. Key events in the continuing atavistic story show that little has altered since the assassination of Greece's first pro-Russian leader, Count Capodistrias, other than cosmetically.

In 1841, the British Minister to Greece, Sir Edmund Lyons, said (see Chapter 1): 'A truly independent Greece is an absurdity. Greece can either be English or Russian, and since she cannot be Russian, it is necessary that she be English'.[42] His words show that the Cold War began long before the so-called Truman Doctrine. In fact, as I mentioned earlier, one can pre-date the beginning of a Cold War mentality to 1791, when the English Prime Minister, William Pitt the Younger, lambasted Russia for wishing to dismember Anatolia. This was only some twenty-two years after Catherine the Great's attempt to free Greece via the Orlov brothers. At any rate, when Greece's first leader, the pro-Russian Capodistrias (a former Russian foreign minister), was assassinated in 1831, Britain breathed a sigh of relief. Thenceforth, Greece was a mere geopolitical tool of the world's largest empire. The Crimean War demonstrates *par excellence* Britain's insistence on keeping Russia away from Greece, just as does Britain's obtaining Cyprus in 1878, whereby Britain undertook to support the Ottoman Empire against Russia. Fast-forward to 1944 when, despite Churchill's 'percentages agreement' with Stalin, whereby Greece would be ten per cent Russian and ninety English, Britain was still highly suspicious of its 'ally' Russia, even though the Foreign Office had admitted that Britain, not the Soviet Union, was responsible for the strength of the Communists in Greece (and Yugoslavia). 1947 is a key year, since this is when Britain literally handed Greece to the US, thus extricating itself from her embarrassing rôle in having aided and abetted the Greek civil war. Britain thus brought America into the Balkans, thereby replacing the dead Austro-Hungarian Empire as its pro-Ottoman and then pro-Turkish friend.

Greece now appears to be again becoming one of the American military and commercial empire's most compliant partners. Let us again go backwards: Trumanesque Greece was firmly part of US and NATO Cold War strategy, with the Left Wing being reviled by the anti-communist deep state which, when threatened by liberalisation, engineered the military coup of 1967, bringing in a particularly pro-American government. Despite the US-condoned invasion of Cyprus which led to the fall of the Junta, Greece's leaving NATO's integrated military structure for a few years, Andreas Papandreou's short-lived push for more independence in foreign policy, and former recent Prime Minister Kostas Karamanlis' attempts to move closer to Moscow (e.g. the abortive Burgas-Alexandroupolis oil pipeline), Greece is now again moving very much into the US/NATO camp, epitomised by the recent signing of the 'EastMed Act', which improves US military co-operation with Greece and establishes areas of co-operation such as energy security in the region, according to Jim Risch, chairman of the US Senate Committee on Foreign Relations.[43] The US is particularly happy with the agreement between Greece, Cyprus and Israel on gas exploration, since it will reduce European dependence on Russian gas. The US is even happier with Prime Minister Mitsotakis' public support for the assassination of Iran's top general, Soleimani, which contrasts with France and Germany's muted response. It is no exaggeration to state that Greece is in many respects emulating the foreign policy of the military dictatorship of 1967–1974.

Another factor in all this is the Greek-American one. There are estimated to be 1,400,000, all with relatives in Greece. As with many immigrants, particularly those who have had to leave their country for economic reasons, many are beholden to their host country's policies, but particularly in the case of policy vis-à-vis Russia. They are spearheaded by the American Hellenic Institute and lobby constantly to try and persuade the US to be firmer with Turkey on the Cyprus question. Yet they are by and large also anti-communist, and therefore anti-Russian, as if the Cold War is uppermost in their minds, with their apparent inability to differentiate between Communism and Russia.

The Greek government seems to think that by making Greece a US military strongpoint, as it has just done, it will gain US support, to help Greece to combat Turkish claims on some Greek islands. This is naïve: the US Embassy has written: 'We recognize Greece's border with Turkey, but not all the territorial waters implications which Greece asserts. We have not taken a position on sovereignty over Imia/Kardak, in part because of the lack of an agreed maritime boundary. We recognize the six [!]-mile territorial sea claim and a claim to the superjacent air space. We do not recognize Greece's claim to territorial air space seaward of the outer limit of its territorial sea'.[44]

Greece can expect no military help from the US, if Turkey invades a Greek island. Indeed, whatever the rhetoric, Turkey is more important to US and NATO interests than Greece. Let us repeat what the FCO wrote in 1975, reflecting US policy then and now: 'We must also recognise that in the final analysis Turkey must be regarded as more important to Western strategic interests than Greece and that, if risks must be run, they should be risks of further straining Greek rather than Turkish relations with the West'.[45] This is still true, whatever the public relations engineering. Greece also seems to have forgotten that the US facilitated and condoned the Turkish invasion of Cyprus. More worrying, Iran has already threatened retaliation, if the US uses any base in Greece to attack it. In diplomacy, detail and precision are more important than pseudo-bonhomie and vague words. Yet, perhaps paradoxically, Greece's behaviour puts Russia in a strong position. Before elaborating on this, let us first look at 'Russian Greece'.

As we have seen, the assassination of Greece's first leader was the first blow to Greece-Russia relations, ushering in a period of instability and foreign, mainly French and British, interference. Yet, as we have seen above, the modern Greek state would not even have come about as it did, were it not for Russia's intervention. Britain was forced to adopt an 'if you can't beat'em, join 'em' approach. Greece was thus able to gain its—albeit qualified—independence, as a protectorate of the 'Powers'. Thereafter, Britain's gunboat 'diplomacy' ensured that Greece was unable to support Russia officially in the Crimean War: Britain simply blockaded Piraeus. But during the Russian Revolution, Greece made a major strategic mistake by fighting the Bolsheviks, to Britain's glee, thus helping Moscow to justify supporting Mustafa Kemal. Although Greece and the Soviet Union were technically on the same side (i.e. the Greek government in exile) following the German invasion of the USSR, the result of the Greek civil war and the Truman Doctrine put paid to any possibility of warm relations between Athens and Moscow. Stalin's internal exiling of around 50,000 Soviet Greeks eastwards should be seen in this context. Thereafter, the banning of the Greek Communist Party in Greece and the military Junta of 1967–1974 put paid to serious relations between Athens and Moscow. Since then, any serious attempts to improve relations have been thwarted in one way or another. Perhaps understandably, Moscow has considerable difficulty in trusting Greek governments, given Greece's NATO-friendly energy policy, such as the US-sponsored Greece-Cyprus-Israel triangle, and now the military agreement with the US.

Therefore, whatever the natural historical atavistic affinity between the Greek and Russian peoples—viz., inter alia, the Cyrillic alphabet, Orthodox Christianity, the Treaty of Küçük Kainardji (whereby Russia won the right to protect Christians in the Ottoman Empire), a commercial treaty granting Greek ships the protection of the Russian flag, the establishment of a military academy for Greeks in Russia, the Greek Battalion of Balaclava (part of the Russian Imperial Army), and the pro-Russian Capodistrias—strategic reality has to date proved stronger than nostalgia, emotion and atavistic affinity.

On top of this, from a purely strategic viewpoint, Turkey is more important to Russia than Greece, one of the most obvious reasons being the fact that the Bosphorus Straits are on Turkish territory, and that Russia values its rights of passage. As Russia has seen Greece being used increasingly by the US as a tool to frustrate various Russian interests in the Eastern Mediterranean, so she has been skilfully playing on Turkish sensitivities to build up its influence. The sale of the S-400 system to Turkey, to Washington's irritation, is a prime example. Moscow has understood that unlike Greece, it can influence events, and chip away at US and NATO interests via Turkey: *Realpolitik* and soft power *par excellence*.

No consideration of Greece-Russia relations can be complete without some reference to Cyprus. The days of Archbishop Makarios' balanced relations with Moscow are dead and gone. Although Russia has taken various initiatives, such as proposing an international conference on Cyprus, NATO and the EU have resisted this, since Russian proposals to rid the island of foreign armed forces are anathema to the US and Britain, who would then have to give the British 'Sovereign Base Areas' to Cyprus, thus weakening NATO's de facto base linking the Eastern Mediterranean to the Middle East. For NATO, Turkish interests take precedence over Cypriot and Greek ones. When Moscow tested the waters by selling its S-300 system to Cyprus in 1997, the resulting Turkish threats and EU and US pressure on Cyprus not to activate the system in Cyprus, saw it transferred to Crete. Again, Turkish interests took precedence. Russia does of course have its red line: when a resolution on the Annan unification plan was discussed in 2004, Russia vetoed it, since the plan as a whole was essentially NATO- (and Turkey-) friendly.

Russia's foreign policy is not by nature aggressive, as the US's and Turkey's tend to be. In the case of its relations with Greece, Moscow is happy to watch Greek-Turkish tensions causing problems for NATO, and influence Turkish foreign policy in the Middle East to suit its own aims of stability. In this respect, Greece is on the sidelines, now considered to be a mere tool of US policy, whereas Turkey has shown some measure of independence vis-à-vis the US, which Greece cannot countenance, perhaps sensing that were Turkey to snatch a Greek island, the US would simply issue a critical statement against Turkey, yet prevent a war between NATO 'allies' Greece and Turkey, just as occurred with the Cyprus crisis in 1974. It wishes to keep its base at Incirlik.

Then becomes now, albeit with different colours. Just as with Britain during her heyday, Greece's relations with Russia today are predicated on the US's keeping Russia at bay in the Eastern Mediterranean and therefore from having positive and close relations with Greece, Russia's natural ally in the nineteenth century. Guicciardini would know.

We can now make a number of observations about geopolitics and how it is practised through geostrategy. First, we need to bear in mind that although the term is little more than one hundred years old, its practice—geostrategy and the application of geopolitics—is as old as Mankind. What geopolitics seeks to describe, analyse, evaluate and advocate is not in the least new. It is simply politically motivated geographers and military people re-inventing the wheel by stating the obvious in new terms. Take Thucydides, for example: although he was more of a recorder of history than a geopolitical man, some of what he describes in his *History of the Peloponnesian War* is germane, particularly regarding geographical position: 'Athens herself would be stronger in relation to Corinth and to the other naval Powers. Then, too, it was the fact that Corcyra lay very conveniently on the coastal route to Italy and Sicily'.[46]

Since the invention of maps, strategic geopolitical considerations have been increasingly important in relations between states (whether pre-or post-Westphalian),[47] especially in war. Although many wars have been labelled dynastic or religious, it was land, resources and trade that often lay behind the overt reasons: the Crusades, theoretically fought for religious reasons, degenerated into land-grabbing, while Bush's 'humanitarian' and 'moral' attack on Iraq (he even mentioned a 'crusade') was to a large extent about oil.

There is nothing new about geopolitics, other than the term, and attempts to make it academically respectable. Over two hundred years ago, Napoleon Bonaparte stated the obvious, when he said that any state makes its politics to suit its geography.[48] What is new is the word and its various semantic refinements and sub-divisions, to take into account modern technology and new resources. Its cold and mechanistic way of approaching relations between states may be accurate and a reflection of the outcome of human characteristics and motives, but those motives and characteristics themselves are swept under the carpet; thus it downplays the true ingredients of relations between states, namely the human factor. Geography has been wrenched from the hands of pure geographers and remoulded by political scientists. The boundaries between military strategy and geostrategy are becoming increasingly blurred, particularly within the context of power politics/political realism. Geopolitics is now rooted in military strategy, with an emphasis on dominating areas of the world, which can be seen as imperialism by another name. Again, Guicciardini's views come to mind.

The geopolitical mindset can serve as an excuse to march in tandem with the darker and more selfish side of business and financial interests, which in turn further feeds the pursuit for power and domination, both individual and corporate. Looking at maps is easier than spending hard mental hours hunting, locating, ravishing, analysing and evaluating original documents, and then trying to understand and write history. Let us have the last word by repeating Christopher Hill: 'The random way in which frontiers are superimposed on the world means that states vary enormously in size, mineral wealth, access to the sea, vulnerability and cohesiveness'.[49]

Before elaborating on geohistory, let us turn to some products of the geopolitical mentality, namely Cyprus and Iraq.

Notes

1. According to Ioannis Mazis of the National and Kapodistrian University of Athens, geostrategy is political intervention to transform or intensify the results of geopolitical analysis.
2. For example, the British Ambassador to Greece, David Madden, spoke to students at New York College, in the run-up to the attack on Iraq, about the 'forces of good'—meaning the British, Americans and their partners. Such puerile and simplistic language hardly becomes an educated diplomat. See op. cit., Mallinson, *William, Cyprus, Diplomatic History and the Clash of Theory in International Relations*, pp. 41 and 197.
3. Orwell, George, 'Politics and the English Language', *Horizon*, London, 1946.
4. Christie, Agatha, *The ABC Murders*, Pan Books, London, 1958 (first published in 1936), p. 162.
5. Guicciardini, Francesco, Counsels and Reflections, translated from the Italian (Ricordi Politici e Civili) by Ninian Hill Thomson, M.A., Kegan Paul, Trench Trübner & Co., Ltd., London, 1890, 82, pp. 39 and 40.

6. Evans, Graham and Newnham, Jeffrey, *The Penguin Dictionary of International Relations*, Penguin, London etc., 1998, p. 197.
7. *The Concise Oxford Dictionary*, Clarendon Press, Oxford, Eighth Edition, 1990.
8. Ioannis Mazis, *Interview* with William Mallinson, Athens, 30 May 2006.
9. Gat, Azar, *The Origins of Military Thought*, Oxford University Press, UK, 1989, pp. 242–243.
10. Presentation to the Senate Armed Services Committee, Subcommittee on Airland Forces, United States Senate, 8 March 2016. Reported on *Russia Today*, in an article entitled 'Russia and China closing in: US fears losing air dominance to more capable adversaries', 12 March 2016.
11. Mahan, Alfred Thayer, *The Problem of Asia and the Effects Upon International Politics*, Konikat Press, Washington and London, 1920, pp. 25–27, 167–168 and 172.
12. Wallbank, T. Walter et al. (eds.), *Civilisation, Past and Present*, volume II, HarperCollins, 1996.
13. Mackinder, Halford, 'The Geographical Pivot of History,' *Geographical Journal*, vol. 23, no. 4, London, April 1904, pp. 421–437.
14. Ó Tuathail, Gearóid, Dalby, Simon and Routledge, Paul, *The Geopolitics Reader*, Routledge, London and New York, 1998, p. 16.
15. Op. cit., Mackinder, 'The Geographical Pivot of History'.
16. Op. cit., Ó Tuathail, Gearóid, 'Introduction', *The Geopolitics Reader*, pp. 17–18. He refers to Mackinder's *Democratic Ideals and Reality: A Study in the Politics of Reconstruction*, Constable and Company Ltd., London, 1919.
17. Huttenback, Robert A., *Racism and Empire*, Cornell University Press, Ithaca and London, 1976, p. 15.
18. Ibid., p. 16.
19. Irving, David, *Churchill's War*, vol. 1, Arrow Books, London, 1989, p. 20. Irving quotes from an article by Churchill from the *Illustrated Sunday Herald* of 8 February 1920, entitled 'Zionism versus Bolshevism: A Struggle for the Soul of the Jewish People'.
20. Neapolitan author of *The New Science*.
21. His later life was somewhat unfortunate. He was upset over Germany's attack on the Soviet Union, since that went entirely against his advice. His having a half-Jewish wife may also have caused him some embarrassment. He and his wife committed suicide in 1946.
22. *Encyclopaedia Britannica*.
23. I consider that the first two world wars were the Seven Years' War and the Napoleonic War(s).
24. Spykman, Nicholas John, *The Geography of the Peace*, Harcourt, Brace and Company, New York, 1944.

25. See Brzezinski, Zbigniew, *The Grand Chessboard: American Primacy and Its Geopolitical Imperatives*, Basic Books, New York, 1997. The title says it all. For a masterly critique of Brzezinski's ideas, see Fouskas, Vassilis K., *Zones of Conflict*, Pluto Press, London, Sterling, Virginia, 2003.
26. Malashenko, Igor, 'Russia: The Earth's Heartland', *International Affairs*, Moscow, Issue 7, July 1990, p. 52. Malashenko quotes from Brzezinski's 'Game Plan: A Strategic Framework for the Conduct of the U.S.-Soviet Contest', *Atlantic Monthly*, Boston and New York, 1986, p. XIV.
27. Hill, Christopher, *The Changing Politics of Foreign Policy*, Palgrave Macmillan, Basingstoke, 2003, p. 133.
28. Op. cit., Ó Tuathail, p. 1.
29. Kissinger, Henry, *Diplomacy*, Simon & Schuster Paperbacks, New York, 1994, p. 21.
30. Ibid.
31. Wight, Martin, in Mallinson, William, *Kissinger and the Invasion of Cyprus*, Cambridge Scholars Publishing, Newcastle upon Tyne, 2016, 2017, p. 178
32. Taylor, A.J.P., *Europe: Grandeur and Decline*, Penguin Books, London, New York etc., 1967 (first published in three volumes, 1950, 1952 and 1956), pp. 22, 24, 25.
33. Solovyev, Eduard G., 'Geopolitics in Russia—Science or Vocation?' *Communist and Post-Communist Studies*, 1 March 2004, vol. 37, issue 1, *research article*.
34. Dugin, Alexandr, *Foundations of Geopolitics*, Arctogaia, Moscow, 1997, in Fellows, Grant Scott, *The Foundation if Alexandr Dugin's Geopolitics*, 1 January 2018, University of Denver, *MA thesis presentation*. I have improved Scott's translation.
35. Op. cit., Hill. P. 168.
36. Op. cit., Ó Tuathail, p. 312.
37. But certainly not exclusively; Mahan, for example, was primarily a naval strategist.
38. Op. cit., Hill, Christopher, p. 168.
39. Ibid.
40. Op. cit., Guicciardini, *Ricordi*, 318, p. 134.
41. Kasli, Shelley, 'Great Game and Partitioning of Syria', *Oriental Review.com*, 19 March 2016.
42. Op. cit., Clogg.
43. *Ekathimerini.com*, 11 January 2020.
44. Mallinson, William, *Cyprus: A Modern History*, I.B. Tauris, London and New York, 2005, 2009, 2012, p. 151.
45. 'British interests in the Eastern Mediterranean', *paper* prepared by Western European Department, FCO, 11 April 1975, FCO 46/1248, file DPI/516/1.

46. Thucydides, *History of the Peloponnesian War*, translated by Rex Warner, introduction and notes by M.I. Finlay, Penguin Books, London etc., 1972, p. 62.
47. I find this term slightly arbitrary and simplistic, but use it, since most IR people have been taught that 1648 was a year of huge significance, in that certain states were created as 'sovereign'; that the principle of non-interference was introduced; and that the power of the Holy Roman Empire was reduced. I discuss this in more depth in my final chapter.
48. Op. cit., Malashenko, note 1, p. 54.
49. Op. cit., Hill, Christopher, p. 169.

Bibliography

Brzezinski, Zbigniew, *The Grand Chessboard: American Primacy and Its Geopolitical Imperatives*, Basic Books, New York, 1997.

Clogg, Richard, *A Concise History of Greece*, Cambridge University Press, 1992.

Christie, Agatha, *The ABC Murders*, Pan Books, London, 1958 (first published in 1936).

Dugin, Alexandr, *Foundations of Geopolitics*, Arctogaia, Moscow, 1997.

Evans, Graham and Newnham, Jeffrey, *The Penguin Dictionary of International Relations*, Penguin, London etc., 1998.

Fouskas, Vassilis K., *Zones of Conflict*, Pluto Press, London, Sterling, Virginia, 2003.

Gat, Azar, *The Origins of Military Thought*, Oxford University Press, UK, 1989.

Guicciardini, Francesco, *Counsels and Reflections*, translated from the Italian (*Ricordi Politici e Civili*) by Ninian Hill Thomson, M.A., Kegan Paul, Trench Trübner & Co., Ltd., London, 1890.

Hill, Christopher, *The Changing Politics of Foreign Policy*, Palgrave Macmillan, Basingstoke, 2003.

Huttenback, Robert A., *Racism and Empire*, Cornell University Press, Ithaca and London, 1976.

Irving, David, *Churchill's War*, vol. 1, Arrow Books, London, 1989.

Kasli, Shelley, 'Great Game and Partitioning of Syria', *Oriental Review.com*, 19 March 2016.

Kissinger, Henry, *Diplomacy*, Simon & Schuster Paperbacks, New York, 1994.

Mackinder, Halford, 'The Geographical Pivot of History,' *Geographical Journal*, vol. 23, no. 4, London, April 1904.

Malashenko, Igor, 'Russia: The Earth's Heartland', *International Affairs*, Moscow, Issue 7, July 1990.

Mallinson William, *Cyprus: Diplomatic History and the Clash of Theory International Relations*, I. B. Tauris, London and New York, 2010.

Mallinson, William, *Kissinger and the Invasion of Cyprus*, Cambridge Scholars Publishing, Newcastle upon Tyne, 2016, 2017.

Mallinson, William, *Cyprus: A Modern History*, I.B. Tauris, London and New York, 2005, 2009, 2012.

Mahan, Alfred Thayer, *The Problem of Asia and the Effects upon International Politics*, Konikat Press, Washington and London, 1920.

Ó Tuathail, Gearóid, Dalby, Simon and Routledge, Paul, *The Geopolitics Reader*, Routledge, London and New York, 1998.

Orwell, George, 'Politics and the English Language', Horizon, London, 1946.

Solovyev, Eduard G., 'Geopolitics in Russia—Science or Vocation?' *Communist and Post-Communist Studies*, 1 March 2004, vol. 37, issue 1.

Spykman, Nicholas John, *The Geography of the Peace*, Harcourt, Brace and Company, New York, 1944.

Taylor, A.J.P., *Europe: Grandeur and Decline*, Penguin Books, London, New York etc., 1967 (first published in three volumes, 1950, 1952 and 1956).

Thucydides, History of the Peloponnesian War, translated by Rex Warner, introduction and notes by M.I. Finlay, Penguin Books, London etc., 1972.

Wallbank, T. Walter et al. (eds.), *Civilisation, Past and Present*, volume II, HarperCollins, 1996.

CHAPTER 5

Casualties of Geopolitics

Abstract This chapter is a case study on how geopolitics has affected Cyprus and Iraq. Both can be identified as entities going back several thousand years, with the Mycenaean Greeks in the case of Cyprus and the Sumerians in Iraq. In their turbulent histories, both have been overrun by different powers, culminating with Turkish and British control in both respectively, before recently becoming theoretically sovereign states. It is interesting to juxtapose them, because they are entirely different entities, one an island and the other a large landmass. The same characteristics of the geopolitical mentality appear to have affected the countries adversely.

Keywords Iraq · Oil · Ottomans · Cyprus · Geopolitics

Borders are scratched across the hearts of men by strangers with a calm judicial pen.[1]

INTRODUCTION

Both Cyprus and Iraq can be identified as entities going back a few thousand years, with the Mycenaean Greeks in the case of Cyprus and the Sumerians in Iraq. In their turbulent histories, both have been overrun by different powers, culminating with Turkish and British control in both

© The Author(s), under exclusive license to Springer Nature Switzerland AG 2021
W. Mallinson, *Guicciardini, Geopolitics and Geohistory*, Palgrave Studies in International Relations, https://doi.org/10.1007/978-3-030-76537-8_5

respectively, before recently becoming theoretically sovereign states. Both were victims of border problems—Iraq with Iran and Kuwait, and Cyprus because of its forced de facto partition. They have also been seen by Britain as strategically connected, given Cyprus' geographical position in the Middle East. A cynic might even claim that they are modern children of imperial geopolitics and power politics rolled into one. Juxtaposing two different geographical entities within a geopolitical context is interesting, in that certain geohistorical parallels can be drawn. Behind British and American strategy vis-á-vis Cyprus and Iraq lies the geopolitical obsession with the Soviet Union and then Russia. Both were held by Britain to stave off what was seen as Russian, and then Soviet, influence, and both were to suffer. In the case of Cyprus, the island was obtained because of British fear of Russia, and in the case of Iraq, even after its theoretical independence in 1932, it became a signatory to the Middle East Treaty Organisation (Baghdad Pact) of 1955, designed, like NATO, to combat a perceived Soviet threat.

Cyprus as a Strategic Cat's Paw

For a geopolitician, Cyprus—nominally sovereign since 1960—has long been a strategic location, *à la* Gibraltar or Diego Garcia, situated in the Eastern Mediterranean, close to Turkey but not far from Syria, Lebanon and Israel. Settled by Greeks in the second millennium BC, the population has remained mainly Greek by language, culture, religion and blood, despite the island having changed hands on numerous occasions. It has been successively controlled by Mycenaean Greeks, Phoenicians, Assyrians, Egyptians, Persians, Macedonian Greeks, Romans, Byzantines, Franco-English (Richard Coeur de Lion), Franks, Venetians, Turks (Ottomans) and British. The Ottomans settled Turks on the island: apart from an influx of Turkish soldiers, many janissaries[2] were also settled on the island, an example of how an imperial geopolitical mentality can include ethnic manipulation[3] (Fig. 5.1).

Cyprus is the only country of the European Union which does not have full sovereign control of its own foreign policy, as the 1960 treaties establishing the republic illustrate. This is a clear example of what Guicciardini meant when he said that the same things return with different colours. Here, we are talking about control by outside powers. The answer to understanding why can be found in a geohistorical approach,

Fig. 5.1 Dependence, illustration by the artist David Mallinson

the main theme of which is today Britain's atavistic preoccupation with Russian power, which still lurks under the surface.[4]

Largely because of her geopolitical fixation with the 'world island', Britain stepped into the strategic merry-go-round in 1877, some twenty years after the Crimean War. By this time, the Ottoman Empire was crumbling, but heavily supported by Britain, as a bulwark against Russia, not unlike today. The British Prime Minister at the time wrote to Queen Victoria: 'If Cyprus can be conceded to your majesty by the Porte, and England at the same time enters into defensive alliance with Turkey, guaranteeing Asiatic Turkey from Russian invasion, the power of England in the Mediterranean will be absolutely increased in that region and your Majesty's Indian Empire immensely strengthened. Cyprus is the key of Western Asia'.[5]

Therefore, during the Congress of Berlin in 1878, held partly because Britain did not like the strengthening of Russia and concomitant weakening of the Ottoman Empire resulting from the Treaty of San Stefano the previous year, she negotiated secretly with the Ottomans. In return for Cyprus, Britain would protect the Ottomans from Russia. The flailing Ottomans succumbed and, to the anger of the French in particular, Cyprus came under British administration, with Britain writing off part of the Ottoman debt, in lieu of paying rent. When Turkey entered the Great War on the side of the Central Powers, Britain annexed Cyprus, declaring it a Crown Colony in 1925. By the Treaty of Lausanne, Turkey renounced all claims to territories under its former jurisdiction.

Union with Greece has been increasingly on the minds of most Cypriots since the outbreak of Greece's war of independence against the Ottoman Empire.[6] At its somewhat constrained independence from Britain in 1960, following an armed liberation and *enosis*[7] struggle that began on April Fools' Day 1955, led by a Cypriot-born Greek Army officer, Grivas, some 18% of the population was described as Turkish Cypriots and the rest as Greek Cypriot, bar a tiny number of Armenians and Maronites. The path to becoming a republic had been fraught with difficulties due, to a considerable extent, to backstage British collusion with Turkey and the Turkish Cypriots, even to the extent of helping them with their propaganda.[8] The objective was to divide the population— Greece and Turkey—so as to make it easier to hang on to the island.[9] The Ministry of Defence's (MOD) view was unequivocal: 'British influence and prestige in the Middle East could not be maintained without the retention of our present military position in Cyprus, which was therefore essential. The denial of our present facilities in Cyprus would mean the complete breakdown of all plans for the development of any Middle East defence organisation and would prevent us from fulfilling our Treaty obligations towards Iraq and Jordan'.[10]

Apart from secretly colluding with the Turkish government and helping it with its propaganda, Britain's objective was to give Turkey a stake in Cyprus, even though this was expressly forbidden by the Treaty of Lausanne. According to Article 16, the new Republic of Turkey was to have no rights in territories under the former jurisdiction of the Ottomans. Britain nevertheless brought Turkey into the Cyprus question, with ill-fated consequences. She invited Greece and Turkey to a conference on 'political and defence questions in the Eastern Mediterranean, including Cyprus'. The Permanent Under-Secretary of the Foreign Office wrote: 'I have always been attracted by the idea of a 3 Power Conference, simply because I believe that it would seriously embarrass the Greek Government. And if such a conference were held, I should not produce any British plan or proposal until a Greek-Turkish deadlock has been defined'.[11]

The conference predictably broke down and was followed by massive anti-Greek rioting in Turkey and the end of the cool but correct Greek-Turkish relations established in 1930 by Greek Premier Venizelos and Turkish President Kamal Atatürk. Britain bears considerable responsibility for the abysmal state of Greek-Turkish relations today.

The qualified independence of 1960 entailed Britain annexing[12] 99 square miles of Cypriot territory (which it keeps to this day), in the shape of the Sovereign Base Areas (SBAs), retaining various sites, overflying rights and rights of passage. The SBAs house the electronic eavesdropping stations that were transferred from Suez. The whole arrangement was predicated on three interrelated treaties of Establishment (over half of which was devoted to the SBAs), Alliance and Guarantee. The package gave the Turkish Cypriots more influence than their 18% presence merited (e.g. 30% of Civil Service posts). The minority could apply the veto in the areas of foreign policy, defence, internal security and taxation. The treaties detracted from the idea of a unitary state based on equal rights. They reflected a range of outside interests that bore little relation to the rights of the Cypriots, namely the US-British interest in maintaining the SBAs for strategic Cold War purposes; the perceived need to keep Cyprus NATO-friendly; and Greek and Turkish interests in maintaining their interests (in dangerous competition with each other, into the bargain). The somewhat convoluted and unique legal package was, on the face of things, intended to work properly, but even the Foreign Office later admitted that the Treaty of Guarantee was contrary to Article 2.4 of the UN Charter, and overridden by Article 103.[13] The intricacy of the whole somewhat convoluted arrangement reflected a compromise between a range of outside interests that had little to do with proper independence, even though Cyprus became a member of the United Nations. In many respects, the 1960 arrangement was a blueprint for further partition, as was to be proven by later events. This was geopolitics in full swing.

Britain, Greece and Turkey had left an important job undone: the question of the separate municipalities. The communities were unable to agree, and President Makarios, with the help of the FO and the British High Commissioner, proposed thirteen amendments to the constitution.[14] The Turkish government got wind of it, and anti-Greek rioting broke out in major towns of Cyprus, leading to a strong Greek Cypriot backlash and the breakdown of the constitution. The Turkish Cypriots unilaterally set up enclaves, resulting in further radicalisation by extremist elements. The cost to Greece was the expulsion of most of the 12,000 Greek nationals residing in Turkey and 60,000 Turkish citizens of Greek stock living in Istanbul and on the islands of Imbros and Tenedos. The Greek government chose not to reciprocate in the case of the thousands of Moslems of Turkish stock living in Western Thrace, who thrive there to this day. To Turkish chagrin, the United Nations then entered the scene.

The tension continued, and the next crisis was in 1967, when Grivas and his soldiers were forced to leave Cyprus, and the de facto division remained. By 1974, the tension had reached fever pitch, with a pro-*enosis* junta in Athens planning a coup against President Makarios, a coup which ended in the Turkish invasion and occupation of over one-third of the island, the declaring of an unrecognised (except by Turkey) state in the northern part of the island, and a stalemate since then. Britain did not fulfil her Treaty of Guarantee obligations and succumbed to Henry Kissinger's pressure to give the Turks free rein.[15] When Britain tried to give up its bases, Kissinger simply pressurised them into keeping them.[16] Turkey has imported many thousands of settlers, altering the natural demography of the island and rendering a just settlement extremely difficult. All manner of attempts have been made until today to unite the island, and all have failed.[17]

Perhaps the most telling recent development was Cyprus' accession on 1 May 2004 to the European Union. The opening of accession negotiations between Cyprus and the EU in 1998 had been highly unwelcome to the Turkish government, since it was itself trying to gain entry, with the strong support of its main sponsors, Britain and the US. Pressure for a settlement increased, since it was obvious that Turkey was in an embarrassing position. A positive gesture was the opening by the occupation regime of some checkpoints, enabling Greek and Turkish Cypriots to cross the buffer zone. The so-called Annan re-unification plan was put to a referendum shortly before Cyprus' formal accession to the EU. The Greek Cypriots rejected it overwhelmingly, while the settlers and the dwindling group of Turkish Cypriots accepted it. It would, in the eyes of many, have legitimised the invasion and occupation, dissolved the republic without strict guarantees for a viable replacement and have maintained the unworkable 1960 treaties.[18] The situation today is somewhat surrealistic, since the whole island is a member of the EU, while the application of the *acquis communautaire* in occupied Cyprus is suspended until the latter is reunited legitimately with free Cyprus. Perhaps even more surrealistic is the fact that Turkey is eager to join the EU, while occupying part of it. It is clear that the US, Britain and Turkey will not permit a truly united and sovereign Cyprus to exist, for fear of Russia. Any solution is therefore predicated on the British bases remaining and on the two main communities being treated as separate entities.

Today's situation is the result of Britain's having stirred up, in the Fifties, extremism among the Turkish Cypriots and in Turkey itself. In the words of Guicciardini: 'The further you depart from the mean course in striving to avoid some extreme, the more likely are you to fall into the extreme you would avoid, or into some other the full as mischievous; and the more intent you are on reaping the fruits of what you actually possess, the sooner will both the possession and your enjoyment of it come to an end'.[19] Since Britain had acted in an extreme manner when the Cypriots began to revolt, she had to give up, at least total, control of Cyprus in 1960. It could, however, be equally well argued that Grivas' rigid nationalist anti-Communist brand of extremism meant that he lacked the flexibility to deal openly with the British authorities and, later, with Makarios himself. Guicciardini's advice is apposite. The personalities of those involved also played a rôle. Guicciardini and geohistory combine here.

A final comment before we turn to Iraq: Greece and Cyprus are inextricably interlinked through atavism, an ingredient of geohistory. At any event, apart from atavism, and given Cyprus' history, we can reasonably state that the island has been characterised by the considerations of big powers/empires biting their fingernails of geostrategic ambition, just as Greece has. As Guicciardini wrote: 'But hateful and pernicious is that ambition which makes self-aggrandisement its sole end and aim, as we find most princes do, who, with this for their goal, and to clear the path that leads to it, put aside conscience, honour, humanity, and all else that is good'.[20]

Whether interests are purely strategic (which today can be virtually synonymous with military, under the euphemistic semantic guise of 'geostrategy') or simply economic (often a more high-sounding word to use than 'commercial'), there has been a good deal of debate about what looks to some like an increasing tendency to merge strategic, business and military interests, to the point where it is sometimes difficult to clearly distinguish between the three. The phenomenon of 'globalisation' (or at least its fuzzy modern version) has surely contributed to this possible merging of interests, as we shall consider in Chapter 7. Let us now become more specific, as we turn to Iraq.

IRAQ AND OIL

The Sykes-Picot Anglo-French deal led to Britain wresting from the Ottoman Empire—after bitter fighting between 1915 and 1917—three provinces, which led, under a British mandate, to the merging of the provinces into an Iraqi state and then kingdom. Although British Petroleum (BP) and the Iraqi élite thrived, very many did not, and various revolts were put down, and in 1932, independence was granted but, as with Cyprus in 1960, it was constrained in terms of sovereignty. In 1958, a violent military anti-monarchist coup (the king was one of many killed) took place, followed by another one, until the Ba'ath Party came to power in 1968, leading to Saddam Hussein's presidency in 1979. From 1958, at any rate, Iraq was more its own master than before, withdrawing from the Baghdad Pact the following year, and was able to get better deals with the oil companies, BP in particular, than hitherto. But the geopolitical machinations of France and Britain had left various border issues between the two countries unresolved, while religion (an Iraqi Sunni leadership versus the Iranian Shi'ites) added its deadly flavour to the cocktail.[21] In 1980, Saddam Hussein attacked Iran, an action condoned by the US, Britain and Israel, who were keen to undermine the new Iranian régime of the Mullahs.

Following the end of the war (in a stalemate) in 1988, Saddam turned his attention to Kuwait—a port whose status had not been properly defined in the Sykes-Picot deal, long claimed by the Ottomans and then Iraq and a British protectorate from 1899 until 1961—invading it in 1990. Saddam appeared to believe that he had American blessing since, a few days before the invasion, the US ambassador, April Glaspie, had assured Saddam that the USA had no interest in Iraq's dispute with Kuwait.[22] Thus, Saddam thought that he had a blank cheque, and invaded, for the US to then perform an about-turn, leading to the Gulf War. Technically speaking, the war had a basis in international law, since Iraq had invaded a nominally sovereign member of the United Nations. Although Bush Senior's aims of ensuring that Iraq would not have control over Kuwait's oil—which constituted 9% of the world's oil reserves[23]— were achieved, his rumbustious aims of creating a 'new world order' and 'kicking the Vietnam syndrome once and for all' were not. It was to be just a question of time before the US invaded Iraq. But when she did, some twelve years later, the attack was illegal and based on a pack of lies. The story is too well known to require analysis here, bar a few points: first,

Bush Junior wanted to finish his father's job; second, the US wished to control Iraq's oil; third, Israel saw Iraq as too powerful for its liking; and fourth, Bush's own personality. In the words of a Poet Laureate: 'Elections, money, empire, oil and Dad'.[24] This was war as a continuation of geopolitics by other means, with a vengeance, and to find any excuse, however false, to invade a country for its oil resources. With Kuwait, Iraq would have held 20% of the world's oil reserves, second only to Saudi Arabia's. This was too much for the US-Israel alliance, surely the closest in the world, despite the geographical distance.

The most recent well-known critique of that alliance was written by respected academics John Mearsheimer and Stephen Walt in 2006,[25] causing a furious reaction among extreme Zionists. The article's main argument was that the power of the Israeli lobby had led to one-sided US support for Israel that was inconsistent with its own interests and those of other states in the region. The power of the Israeli lobby had already been noted, thirty years earlier, albeit in secret, by the British embassy in Washington: 'The well-organised lobby of Jewish organisations concentrates its activities on influencing congress. There is very little activity in State Legislatures, mainly because few issues arise affecting Israel or the Jewish community in those bodies. The obvious point of pressure must be Congress and there is little doubt that much of the active output of the Zionist organisations is devoted to that end [...] whenever an important event occurs in the world at large or in this country, or whenever there is any public threat to Israel, a flood of letters descends upon the offices of Senators and Representatives throughout the country. Some, no doubt, are spontaneous, but the majority show unmistakable evidence of a careful orchestration'.[26] The paper added: 'A well-known columnist, who writes in the Christian Science Monitor, told us last year that, when he wrote an editorial which contained mild criticism about the intransigence of the Israeli government, he received a telephone call from the Israeli Embassy in Washington within the hour to express official Israeli displeasure. He was told that such judgements would not be well received by many of the big firms in the Boston area who bought advertising space in the paper and that the Israeli Embassy were confident that he would not wish to deprive his paper of much needed revenue. [...] There can be little doubt that the Israeli Embassy discreetly passes on information to the Jewish organisations, but it would be difficult to point to a direct link'.[27]

When geopolitical fundamentalism merges with propaganda and emotion, along with illegality, it can be a deadly cocktail, and there can be reactions. For example, in Britain, the Father of the House of Commons, Tam Dalyell, sparked anger among extremist Jewish groups when he said that the then Prime Minister, Blair, relied too much on Jewish figures, naming controversial Middle East Adviser Lord Levy and former Minister and then EU Trade Commissioner Peter Mandelson. Even more dangerously, Dalyell referred to a 'cabal of Jewish advisers' in the US, naming the controversial Paul Wolfowitz[28] (then Deputy Defense Secretary), Richard Perle (adviser) and Ari Fleischer (Bush's then Press Secretary), among others. He alluded to the 'neo-Christian fundamentalist co-operation with Zionists' and decried the 'extreme Likudnik agenda'.[29] He also made plain to this author his view that Mossad had been instrumental in drumming up false stories about the Iraqi régime trying to obtain uranium from Niger.[30] Even respected writers like John Le Carré weighed in: 'Your little Prime Minister is not the American President's *poodle*, he is his *blind dog* [...] Supported by Britain's *servile corporate media*, he has given *spurious respectability to American imperialism*. [...] And since the so-called coalition, by making an unprovoked attack on Iraq, has already broken *half the rules in the international law books, and intends by its continued occupation of Iraq to break the other half*, should we not be insisting that the principal instigators be forced to account for themselves before the International Courts of Justice in The Hague?'[31] Yet more damningly, the war journalist John Pilger recently wrote: 'Their response surprised me. Had "we," they said – that is journalists and broadcasters, especially in the U.S. — challenged the claims of the White House and Downing Street, investigated and exposed the lies, instead of amplifying and echoing them, the invasion of Iraq in 2003 probably would not have happened. Countless people would be alive today. Four million refugees would not have fled. The grisly ISIS, a product of the Blair-Bush invasion, might not have been conceived'.[32]

In sum, it is reasonable to conclude that the Sykes-Picot arrangement to divide the Middle East into British and French spheres of influence was the seed that would lead a few years later to the birth of the modern Middle East and the concomitant decades of political turmoil, wars, sectarian killing, socio-economic disparities and the interminable Arab-Israel conflict: geopolitics at its worst.

STRATEGY, GREED AND OIL

Although Cyprus had no oil, the island was unable to escape the nefarious influence of the oil game, as the British Prime Minister, Eden, put it so succinctly: 'No Cyprus, no certain facilities to protect our supply of oil. No oil, unemployment and hunger in Britain. It's as simple as that'.[33] It was Cyprus' geographical position that led to its being a geopolitical football, as a British, and then American and British, strategic asset in the old 'Great Game' against Russia, the Soviet Union and now Russia again, and to protect the transit of oil to Britain. The Suez crisis had of course occasioned the transfer of Britain's Middle Eastern strategic (read military) interests to Cyprus. The subtle geopolitician *par excellence* Henry Kissinger recognised this at the time: 'But for the foreseeable future we should be able to count on [...] Cyprus or Libya as staging areas for the Middle East, and on Great Britain as a staging area for Europe'.[34] Some years later, the FCO wrote of Kissinger: Dr. Kissinger has frequently spoken of the value of this 'real estate' and the necessity to keep it as a 'British square on the chequer board',[35] and 'He was also concerned with the effects of United States policy over Cyprus on the resolution of the Arab/Israel problem, and he regarded this as more important than Greek hostility towards the United States, despite the effect of this dissension on the Southern Flank of the Alliance'.[36]

Just as Cyprus is a pertinent example of the effects of geostrategy, so Iraq provides us with an effective example of the dangers of an unbridled geopolitical approach: as a result of the attack on Iraq, the Iraqis nowadays consider themselves to be more Shia, Sunni or Kurdish than simply Iraqi. State consciousness, so important in keeping people together, is no longer the order of the day.

The way in which geopolitical considerations have negatively affected the well-being of Iraq has had a negative impact on the region and the world, but been good for certain businesses. President Eisenhower's warning about the military-industrial complex has not been heeded.[37]

The invasion of Kuwait was a vivid reminder that the most elemental components of geopolitical power are still very much a part of the international system, especially in the Middle East and Cyprus.[38] Guicciardini would surely agree. As with politics, economic confrontation can be considered as continuation of war by other means. The terminology may change as well as the arena, but the adversaries, as well as the goal for domination and power, remain.

With the war in Iraq, the US wanted to achieve two objectives: economic hegemony over the vast oil fields of Iraq and political control, by toppling a 'defiant dictator' who bullied his neighbours and had made the region unstable. Saddam may have been the most important reason, since before the Gulf War of the early 1990s, his country was on the way to becoming a regional power that would have threatened the security of Israel, the US's most reliable ally in the Middle East, as well as that of Saudi Arabia and the ruling monarchy, the US's strongest Arab ally. It was a case of a 'breakaway country' that had nevertheless been sponsored and armed by the US during the Iran-Iraq War of 1980–1988.

The preparations for the 2003 adventure were made well in advance. Halliburton, a company involved in oil and gas exploration, was asked to prepare a forecast for the worst-case scenario regarding the oil infrastructure and oil wells of Iraq, should Saddam decide to destroy them while retreating from the US army's advance.[39] Halliburton's CEO in the early 1990s was Vice President Dick Cheney, who was scrutinised by the press and the opposition in the US for his ties to the company and for the lucrative contracts he granted it. In Guicciardini's words: 'Prosperity is often our worst enemy, making us vicious, frivolous, and insolent'.[40] 'For greedy men believe easily whatsoever they desire, and simple men know not when they are deceived'.[41]

According to *The Economist*, some investment bankers maintained that the 'likeliest scenario is a short, successful war' which 'might actually be good for the world economy: it will eliminate today's mood of uncertainty, boost government spending, and push oil prices lower in the medium term as new Iraqi production comes on stream'.[42]

The US administration and political analysts who supported the Iraq War supported this view.[43] The war did indeed boost government spending, as can be seen from the effect on the companies selling to the US army and on the oil companies and related businesses. Halliburton's stock price rose substantially after the invasion of Iraq, from 15.8 dollars per share in 2004 to 38.69 in 2008, which can also be seen with the arms companies constituting the military-industrial-congressional complex.[44] But the medium- and long-term effect was catastrophic for Iraq. Let us leave the last word to Guicciardini: 'Wars have no greater peril than that he who has just entered upon them should take their success for certain. For however safe and easy they may seem, they are subject to a thousand accidents, and these will lead to still greater disorder if he whom it concerns is not ready to put forth both strength and courage'.[45]

Following Saddam's ousting and the occupation of Iraq by the US and its allies, the original partners in the Iraq Petroleum Company, Exxon Mobil, Shell, Total and BP, flocked to the country, seeking to regain their concessions for Iraq's oil fields. The exploitation contracts under the auspices of the US occupation would be the first commercial operation since the ousting of these oil companies by Saddam Hussein thirty-six years previously. It is no surprise that these companies, rather than any others, obtained the initial rights to oil and gas exploitation in Iraq: it was a form of shareholders' atavism.

Oil also influenced the attempt to remove Assad in Syria: as we have seen in Chapter 4, John F. Kennedy's nephew and namesake alluded to the US' decision to remove President Assad because he had refused to back a Qatari gas pipeline project.[46]

Conclusions

We have seen how the geopolitical approach, with its warlike geostrategy, focuses essentially on resources and profit, but ignores the fate of human beings. It also appears to thrive, perhaps paradoxically, on a measure of chaos and, more recently, on the globalisation obsession, where speed and greed are having an increasingly symbiotic relationship. The human factor is much ignored in geopolitics, both regarding leaders' own proclivities and the ordinary people whom it affects. Geopolitics also tends to ignore the niceties of international law. Guicciardini, as we have seen, and shall see, puts considerable emphasis on human characteristics and behaviour, as does geohistory, to which, having hinted at its relevance in the preceding chapters, we must now bite the bullet and be specific.

Notes

1. Marya Mannes, in Hitchens, Christopher, 'The Perils of Partition', *The Atlantic*, Boston, March 2003.
2. From the Turkish for 'new soldier', 'yeni çeri'. They had been taken from the Balkans (they were not generally Turks) as boys, made into Moslems and then trained to become the élite guards of the Sultan.
3. The Tamil Tiger revolt in Sri Lanka, for example, can be seen as the result of ethnic manipulation: in the nineteenth century, Britain sent thousands of Tamils from Southern India to Ceylon, to work on the tea plantations. Their descendants were to revolt (Tamil Tigers) against the Sinhalese majority.

4. Mallinson, William, 'Greece and Cyprus as Geopolitical Fodder, and the Russian Connexion', *Journal of Balkan and Near Eastern Studies*, vol. 22, no. 3, April 2020.
5. Buckle, B. E., *The Life of Benjamin Disraeli, Earl of Beaconsfield*, John Murray, London, 1920, p. 291.
6. Paul W. Wallace and Andreas G. Orphanides (eds.), *Sources for the History of Cyprus*, vol. XI, Enosis and the British: British Official Documents 1878–1950, selected and edited by Coughlan, Reed, Greece and Cyprus Research Center, Altamont, Albany, NY, 1990–2004. A reading of this volume quickly dispels the myth, invented by some, that the idea of union with Greece came only very late to Cyprus.
7. Union (with Greece, á la Crete).
8. Bowker to Young, 15 February 1955, *letter*, PRO FO 371/117625, file RG 1081/120.
9. The policy of *divide et impera* is of course not exclusive to Britain.
10. *Memorandum* by (British) Ministry of Defence, 28 June 1955, NA/FO 371/117640, file RG 1081/536. Britain was already planning to move its Middle East Headquarters from Egypt to Cyprus.
11. William Mallinson, 'Turkish Invasions, Britain, Cyprus and the Treaty of Guarantee', *Synthesis, Review of Modern Greek Studies*, vol. 3, no. 1 (1999), 47, in William Mallinson, *Cyprus, a Modern History*, London and New York 2005, 2009, 2010; Kirkpatrick to Nutting, 26 June 1955, minute, PRO FO 371/17640, file RG 1081/535.
12. Some lawyers might argue that, technically speaking, the SBAs were annexed by Britain from its Crown Colony, which was then granted independence.
13. Op. cit., Mallinson, *Cyprus, a Modern History*, pp. 53-6; Moreton to McPetrie, minute, 14 December 1967, and McPetrie's reply, 1 March 1968, PRO 27/166/MF/10/41.
14. Ibid., p. 35. The British rôle is indisputable: in a letter of 13 March 1971 from Secondé (Southern European Department FCO) to Ramsbotham (High Commissioner in Cyprus), the former wrote: 'We have been through the 1963 papers, which tend to confirm that the Thirteen Points were indeed framed with British help and encouragement; that the then High Commissioner [Clark] considered them to be reasonable prospects; and that our intention was to promote their acceptance by the Turks'. Ramsbotham later wrote to Secondé: 'Makarios, ever the gentleman, took sole responsibility for the Thirteen Points'. See also Markides Diana, 'Cyprus 1957–1963; from Colonial Conflict to Constitutional Crisis: the Key Role of the Municipal Issue', Minneapolis, MI, 2001, for an analysis of the 1963 outburst.
15. See Mallinson, William, *Kissinger and the Invasion of Cyprus*, Cambridge Scholars Publishing, Newcastle upon Tyne, 2016, 2017.

16. Mallinson, William, *Cyprus: Diplomatic History and the Clash of Theory International Relations*, I.B. Tauris, London and New York, 2010, pp. 91–94.
17. See Mirbagheri, Farid, *Cyprus and International Peacekeeping*, C. Hurst & Co., London 1998. A well set out and informative book. One of the best on Cyprus' situation.
18. See op. cit., Mallinson, William, *Cyprus, A Modern History*, Chapter Fifteen.
19. Guicciardini, Francesco, *Counsels and Reflections*, translated from the Italian (*Ricordi Politici e Civili*) by Ninian Hill Thomson, MA, Kegan Paul, Trench Trübner & Co., Ltd., London, 1890, 188, p. 83.
20. Ibid., 32, pp. 19–20.
21. In the nineteenth century, the Safavids forced the Iranians to convert to the Shia branch of Mohamedanism. The Iraqi leadership was, however, Sunni.
22. Parenti, Michael, *Inventing Reality*, St. Martin's Press, New York, 1993, p. 164.
23. Dunne, Michael, 'The United States, the United Nations and Iraq', *International Affairs*, vol. 79, no. 2, March 2003, p. 264.
24. Ezard, John, 'Poet Laureate Joins Doubters over Iraq', *The Guardian*, 9 January, 2003, in Dunn, David Hastings, 'Myths, Motivations and 'Misunderstandings': The Bush Administration and Iraq', in ibid., *International Affairs*, p. 279.
25. Mearsheimer, John and Walt, Stephen, 'The Israel Lobby', *London Review of Books*, 23 March 2006.
26. 'Zionist Organisations in the United States', *paper* prepared by the British Embassy in Washington, 16 March 1972, FCO 17/1763, file NER 18/7.
27. Ibid.
28. Wolfowitz was later sacked from his then job as head of the International Monetary Fund, for allegedly giving a girlfriend a rather good job.
29. White, Michael, 'Dalyell Renews Attack on Levy', *The Guardian*, 6 May 2003. Levy, a bit of a seedy character, and close to discredited Prime Minister Anthony Blair, was later arrested and questioned by the police in the 'cash for honours' scandal.
30. Tam Dalyell, telephone interview with author, 17 July 2003.
31. Le Carré, John, *Absolute Friends*, Coronet Books (Hodder and Stoughton), London, 2004, pp. 267–8.
32. Pilger, John, 'The Most Lethal Virus Is Not Covid. It Is War', *MPN NEWS*, 14 December 2020.
33. O'Malley, Brendan and Craig, Ian, *The Cyprus Conspiracy*, I.B. Tauris, London and New York, 1999, p. 7.
34. Kissinger, Henry A., *Nuclear Weapons and Foreign Policy*, Harper and Brothers, New York, 1957, p. 165.

35. Southern European Department to Minister of State, 27 October 1976, BNA/FCO 9/2388, file WSC 023/1, pt. H.
36. 'British Policy on Cyprus: July to September 1974', *paper*, BNA/FCO 9/2379, file WSC 020/548/1.
37. He was advised to delete the word 'congressional' at the last minute, for fear of antagonising a large number of members of Congress.
38. Kemp, Geoffrey and Harkavy, Robert E., *Strategic Geography and the changing Middle East*, Carnegie Endowment for International Peace, Brookings Institute Press, Washington, DC, 1997, pp. xi, xii.
39. *An Oversight Hearing on Waste, Fraud, and Abuse in U.S. Government Contracting in Iraq*, Senate Democratic Policy Committee Hearing, Bunnatine Greenhouse U.S. Army Corps of Engineers, June 27 2005.
40. Op. cit., Guicciardini, Ricordi, 164, p. 73.
41. Ibid., 105, p. 48.
42. 'The Economic Risks', *The Economist*, 22 February 2003, p. 69., noted in Epstein, Rachel A., Vennesson, Pascal (eds.), *Globalization and Transatlantic Security*, Robert Schuman Centre for Advanced Studies, European University Institute, Florence, Italy, July 2006.
43. Byman, Daniel, 'After the Storm: US Policy Toward Iraq Since 1991', *Political Science Quarterly*, vol. 115, no. 4, Winter 2000–2001, pp. 493–516.
44. For a more in-depth view, see Mallinson, William and Ristic, Zoran, *The Threat of Geopolitics to International Relations: Obsession with the Heartland*, Cambridge Scholars Publishing, Newcastle upon Tyne, 2016 and 2017.
45. Op. cit., Guicciardini, Ricordi, 180, p. 79.
46. Kasli, Shelley, 'Great Game and Partitioning of Syria', OrientalReview.com, 19 March 2016.

Bibliography

Byman, Daniel, 'After the Storm: US Policy Toward Iraq Since 1991', *Political Science Quarterly*, vol. 115, no. 4, Winter 2000–2001.

Dunne, Michael, 'The United States, the United Nations and Iraq', *International Affairs*, vol. 79, no. 2, March 2003.

Epstein, Rachel A., Vennesson, Pascal (eds.), *Globalization and Transatlantic Security, Robert Schuman Centre for Advanced Studies*, European University Institute, Florence, Italy, July 2006.

Guicciardini, Francesco, *Counsels and Reflections*, translated from the Italian (*Ricordi Politici e Civili*) by Ninian Hill Thomson, MA, Kegan Paul, Trench Trübner & Co., Ltd., London, 1890.

Hitchens, Christopher, 'The Perils of Partition', *The Atlantic*, Boston, March 2003.
Kasli, Shelley, 'Great Game and Partitioning of Syria', OrientalReview.com, 19 March 2016.
Kemp, Geoffrey and Harkavy, Robert E., *Strategic Geography and the Changing Middle East, Carnegie Endowment for International Peace*, Brookings Institute Press, Washington, DC, 1997.
Kissinger, Henry A., *Nuclear Weapons and Foreign Policy*, Harper and Brothers, New York, 1957.
Le Carré, John, *Absolute Friends*, Coronet Books (Hodder and Stoughton), London, 2004.
Mallinson, William, *Cyprus, a Modern History*, London and New York 2005, 2009, 2010.
Mallinson, William, *Cyprus: Diplomatic History and the Clash of Theory International Relations*, I.B. Tauris, London and New York, 2010.
Mallinson, William, *Kissinger and the Invasion of Cyprus*, Cambridge Scholars Publishing, Newcastle upon Tyne, 2016, 2017.
Mallinson, William, 'Greece and Cyprus as Geopolitical Fodder, and the Russian Connexion', *Journal of Balkan and Near Eastern Studies*, vol. 22, no. 3, April 2020.
Mallinson, William and Ristic, Zoran, *The Threat of Geopolitics to International Relations: Obsession with the Heartland*, Cambridge Scholars Publishing, Newcastle upon Tyne, 2016 and 2017.
Markides Diana, 'Cyprus 1957–1963; from Colonial Conflict to Constitutional Crisis: the Key Role of the Municipal Issue', Minneapolis, MI, 2001.
Mearsheimer, John and Walt, Stephen, 'The Israel Lobby', *London Review of Books*, 23 March 2006.
Mirbagheri, Farid, *Cyprus and International Peacekeeping*, C. Hurst & Co., London 1998.
O'Malley, Brendan and Craig, Ian, *The Cyprus Conspiracy*, I.B. Tauris, London and New York, 1999.
Parenti, Michael, *Inventing Reality*, St. Martin's Press, New York, 1993.
Wallace, Paul W., and Orphanides, Andreas G. (eds.), Sources for the History of Cyprus, vol. XI, Enosis and the British: British Official Documents 1878–1950, selected and edited by Coughlan, Reed, Greece and Cyprus Research Center, Altamont, Albany, NY, 1990–2004.

CHAPTER 6

Geohistory

Abstract This chapter ties together key points made in the previous chapters, setting out and explaining the essential elements of geohistory, first by arguing that history, in the purest form, is the past, which is occurring as we write. In antithesis to theories, with their models, paradigms and conceptual frameworks, geohistory is detached, depending rather on understanding human characteristics, both individual and corporate, which are the starting point of all relations between people and countries. As such, appearances and atavism are vital ingredients.

Keywords Geohistory · History · The past · Models · Human characteristics

ΤΑΠΑΝΤΑΡΕΙ
Heraclitus

INTRODUCTION

By now, the reader will have understood that the various references in the preceding chapters, to both Guicciardini and geohistory, now require some justification and explanation. Geohistory is an approach to understand, analyse and evaluate relations between states, depending closely on

© The Author(s), under exclusive license to Springer Nature
Switzerland AG 2021
W. Mallinson, *Guicciardini, Geopolitics and Geohistory*,
Palgrave Studies in International Relations,
https://doi.org/10.1007/978-3-030-76537-8_6

researching original documents, as Guicciardini advocated. Unlike geohistory, geopolitics has succumbed to a worldview based mainly on the acquiring of resources to maintain and increase the power of a state, hence its connexion to political realism and national interests. The geopolitical approach, so attractive to political realists, has been seen to lead to strife. In this chapter, we shall develop the methods for understanding geohistory. But first, what of history per se? Let us take a look at an almost Guicciardinian view by Christopher Hill.

ONLY HISTORY EXISTS

'The need is to look on history not as a store cupboard of the off-the-shelf-possible solutions, but as something integral to ourselves and our sense of identity in both time and space. If history is looked upon as perpetual flux, with familiar objects bobbing up regularly, the present becomes intimately connected to both past and future. It becomes possible to be aware of both difference and similarity without attempting to follow a particular model'.[1]

Let us now take this further: in its purest form, history is the past. Since all is constantly moving, the 'present' becomes the past as it occurs, and is in reality simply our awareness of what we see, namely what has occurred—in other words our memory. The future cannot exist until it becomes the past: it is simply our expectation and assumption, sometimes influenced by our desires: in Guicciardini's words: 'Most truly has the wise man said that of things future and contingent we can have no certain knowledge. Turn this over in your mind as you will, the longer you turn it the more you will be satisfied of its truth'.[2] Our starting point must therefore be to reduce the definition of history to its simplest form, the past, and, concomitantly, the study of the past, bearing in mind that we need to differentiate between the recording of events as they occur and the interpreting of what has been recorded. Far from slotting thoughts into paradigms, conceptual frameworks and models, geohistory sees geography at its most basic, namely the study of the physical earth and its inhabitants. By adding the word 'history', we then have the study of the Earth's history, with history as a neutral continuum that remains unaffected by any theory. Just as geography has been infected by politics—hence the term 'geopolitics'—so can geography be infected—but benignly—by history. Unlike geopolitics, which has been affected by political ideology, geohistory is politically dispassionate. It can of course enable a detached approach to various ideologies, which are of course themselves part of history, but without fear of itself catching a political virus. Geohistory is immune.

As stated earlier, only history/the past exists. The future cannot exist except in our minds, while the present is always moving into the past and cannot be grasped. As Heraclitus wrote, 'everything flows'. As for what we term 'events', they are merely our view on something that we believe has happened. When we try to interpret, analyse and evaluate events, as is natural to us, different interpretations, often in the form of theories, models and indeed our own experiences, can create dispute. For some common sense, we must turn back to Guicciardini. To his maxim that everything that is and will be has already been in former times, we can add: 'Whence it happens that as the things of this world are subject to infinite changes and chances, in the course of events unlooked-for help may come in many ways to him who has obstinately persevered; which perseverance being the result of faith, it may well be said that whoso hath faith will accomplish great things'.[3]

Giambattista Vico, writing some two hundred years later, argued that perfection could never exist on Earth. Science could never explain the essence of a thing, but only how it is made. His Christianity and implied criticism of Cartesian rationalism must be anathema to many of the behaviourist, and even, in some cases, to the structuralist realist schools, with their attachment to the methodologies of natural science to explain behaviour. For Vico, the study of history was necessary to understand Mankind.[4] Such simplicity of wisdom is difficult to find in modern international relations theory, let alone in geopolitics. The well-known adage that history repeats itself is itself inaccurate, since things can never replicate themselves precisely. Rather, the same kind of events occur, but raise their heads every so often, with different colours. What many theorists and geopoliticians learn from history is simply how to repeat mistakes, rather than how to avoid making them. In a sense, we are but bipedic memories, only rarely considering the implications of our memory in order to avoid strife. We are ourselves history. This is where the crucial ingredients of geohistory come in: human characteristics.

THE HUMAN CONNEXION

It is not, as we have said, that history repeats itself, but that the same things return with different colours. To this, we can add—even if it sounds simplistic—that history is itself humanity or mass bipedic memories. Apart from fortune and the unpredictable, human characteristics determine humanity's fate, just as they do that of an individual. It is to immutable *individual* characteristics and behaviour (often unpredictable) that we must therefore first turn, as the sole earthly criteria of how humans exist. This is very different to the cold and allegedly logical way in which geopolitics approaches relations between states. Although humans invented the term 'geopolitics', they nevertheless ignored the human factor, concentrating on resources and the strategy of obtaining them. Like so much international relations theory, geopolitics appears as an escape route from the actual ingredients of human relations, international included. These ingredients are based on individual, and therefore only by extension, on mass, human behaviour. Geohistory is indeed the very antithesis of geopolitics.

International relations theories are condemned to remain but theories, necessary perhaps as an intellectual tool of academic respectability, used by think tanks to justify various government actions, just as political realism and geopolitics have been used to justify illegal and unilateral attacks. It is quite legitimate to describe the world as consisting of the weak, the weaker and the weakest.[5] Such an idea, despite its slight hint of humour, would attract the out-and-out political realist, even if it were only coined cynically and critically. Yet it may also be true: after all, the first thing that cows usually do when let into a field is to line up. The vast majority of humans tend to form, or join, groups, as the case may be. Perhaps this is part of what Aristotle was implying when he wrote that Man is a political animal.[6] The problem comes with how one interprets human self-organisation, borders and states. We advocate ideology-free geohistory as the approach.

The characteristics that cause strife are manifold. Let us look at some of the basic ones. First must come insecurity. When individuals or groups feel insecure, they sometimes resort to desperate actions. A feeling of insecurity can stem from various factors, perhaps the most basic being a lack of the resources that one needs to survive. A person or group that is in danger of dying through lack of food will automatically tend to put morality on the back-burner when it comes to survival. The instinct for survival tends to forget morality, at least when it comes to life or death. At the most basic individual level, this can mean a mother or father stealing for their children, while at the most extreme group level it can mean invading another country to settle on its territory, or at least to somehow grab its resources. In the latter case, greed is of course a factor. But, natural disasters such as drought and earthquakes apart, countries can often find ways of feeding their inhabitants through, for example, belt-tightening, inventiveness and improved organisation, or even imposing high taxation on the very rich, without having to attack other countries. When insecure, some countries turn to larger ones. For example, Syria turned to Russia and Israel to America. This is where fear comes in. Fear is obviously connected to insecurity, in the sense that the more secure one feels, the less likely it is that one will succumb to fear, and thus to aggression, which is connected to greed.

At an individual level, greed can be the result of insecurity, which then gets out of control, and the habit of acquiring goods and/or money becomes unstoppable. At a state/corporate level, greed translates itself into the selfish part of 'national interests', often in the shape of shareholders' interests. Oil, which we have termed 'black blood', is the most obvious example of mass/state/corporate greed. At the geopolitical level, the secret Anglo-French Sykes-Picot agreements (see above) are a prime example of the artificial creation of dictatorial Middle Eastern states in the interests of their ruling families and of British and French shareholders in oil companies. The borders drawn were imposed more by business interests than those of common ethnographic sense. It is hardly surprising that the Middle East is a combustible (no pun intended) mess today.

This leads us to atavism, an oft-ignored factor in international relations theory, and one almost completely ignored by political geographers. Yet it is vital in understanding people and the states in which they live. Religion can play an important rôle here: within the Yugoslav context, for example, the Bosniaks, who were simply Slavs, converted to Mohammedanism, differentiated themselves from their Christian brothers, and were attacked by both Roman Catholic Croatian Slavs and Christian Orthodox Serb Slavs when the Cold War went into temporary hibernation in 1989. *Au comble de malheur*, the atavistic tendencies of old, namely the clash between Roman Catholics and Christian Orthodox, went into top gear in the Nineties, culminating in NATO's illegal bombing of Serbia in 1999. Had the Vatican itself not atavistically recognised Croatian independence prematurely in 1992 (it was the first state to do so), much subsequent blood-spilling might have been spared. This was the dark side of atavism with a vengeance: Croatia is predominantly Roman Catholic. Had it been Christian Orthodox, it is difficult to imagine the Vatican's indecent haste in recognising Croatia. Again, Guicciardini comes to mind: 'I desire to see [...] the world delivered from the tyranny of these rascally priests'.[7] Apart from religion—and its exploitation through politics—race and language are also important factors in atavism. Individual and national characteristics are based on it. Take Germany and the Germans: both individually and at state level, it is said that an excess of logic, and a concomitant lack of tactility, often prevails. In contrast, Italy and the Italians are more flexible and humane. As for the Greeks, again at both individual and corporate level, they tend to cut corners and even to cheat. These particular atavistic characteristics have their roots in the Ottoman occupation, which lasted for hundreds of years. The whole Greek state is a product of clientelism, which covers all manner of corruption, particularly bribery.

Pride, both individual and corporate, is also a vital and often overlooked factor in international relations theory. Yet it is vital, since face-saving matters in international crises. Often, when faces are not saved, war results. One example was the pride of the governments of Austro-Hungary and Serbia in 1914, following the assassination of the Archduke Ferdinand and his wife. Although the Serb government agreed to nearly all Vienna's demands, it was not prepared to yield vital areas of sovereignty, such as giving Austro-Hungarian officials free rein on Serbian territory. In the same connexion, the Rambouillet accord of 1999 was unacceptable to Belgrade precisely because it would have allowed NATO to operate on Serbian territory. The same things return with different colours. Sometimes, swallowing one's pride can prevent war. Consider Russia's intervention in Syria. The US was undoubtedly embarrassed when Russia exposed American ineptitude, and worse, in Syria. Had a gung-ho John McCain[8] been in power, we could well have witnessed a dangerous escalation leading to a nuclear war. Pride is of course a multifaceted characteristic and can often be connected to insecurity, which can in turn be connected to the problem of identity. Consider the following perceptive comment about Turkey by a British ambassador: 'Leaving aside Istanbul and Izmir and the Aegean littoral, for my money Turkey is more of the Near East and Asia than Europe. Not just physically, with 97 per cent of its territory in Asia, but temperamentally. […] Perhaps this deliberate cultivation of a Western outlook, with all that it means in education, has led the ruling circles and intellectuals and industrialists to regard themselves as truly European, and Turkey in general as Western. […] There is no natural reason why the Turks should be so insistent on their European connexion. […]. Although to speak of an identity crisis would be rather strong, it is certainly arguable that the younger the state, the more the quest to seek an identity'.[9]

Nor can Greece escape from this identity quest. Although its modern state is about twice as old as Turkey's, and although, unlike the Turks, the Greeks were established as a people in the same area about two thousand years before the Turkish tribes even came to Anatolia, the Slavic invasions[10] and the subsequent Ottoman occupation created a modern sense of insecurity, connected to identity. Let us juxtapose Turkey with Greece, again with the help of an ambassador: 'In all its years since modern independence, the Greeks have never quite known where they stood in relation to Europe. They have had a problem of identity'.[11]

To make our point yet more clearly, the Republic of North Macedonia is an example of a new state without a solid identity.[12] Its two main groups are Slavs (Bulgarised Serbs and Serbs) and an almost one-third minority of Albanians, many of whom would like to join Albania. They claim to be descended from the Ancient Macedonians. This is a bizarre claim, since the Slavs arrived in the area around fifteen hundred years after the Greek-speaking Macedonians, who had arrived with the tail-end of the Dorians. As regards the attempt to create a Macedonian language (Alexander the Great and his people spoke Greek), a British Special Operations Executive officer wrote in 1944 that the language was corrupt and debased, without a literature or a fixed grammar.[13] Its language is essentially a form of bastardised Slavonic and has nothing to do with historical Macedonia.[14]

We are simply making the point that as regards geohistory, the younger the state, so the more human characteristics of insecurity, fear and greed come to the fore. When that state is not sufficiently homogenous, and when a majority part of it, in the quest for recognition, feels the need to try and acquire the identity of part of a larger neighbour, we descend to the level of identity crisis.

Apart from the negative corporate characteristics which we have mentioned, reflected in insecurity, fear, pride, aggression and greed, we cannot conclude this chapter before mentioning the importance of appearance.

APPEARANCES

A human being's tendency to show his/her best face is a natural trait of human behaviour, but can be over-exploited when it comes to politics. Guicciardini observes: 'Since a name for goodness will help you in numberless ways, do all you can to seem good. But since false appearances are never lasting, you can hardly succeed in seeming good for long, unless you be so in reality'.[15] This of course connects to reputation: 'Think less of gaining good-will than of maintaining a good reputation. For losing reputation, you lose good-will, in room thereof comes contempt. But he who maintains his reputation shall never lack friends or favour'.[16] In showing us the reality of how to maintain appearance and reputation in public life, Guicciardini by default also shows the difference between public and private behaviour, something well understood by Erving Goffman 450 years later,[17] when he wrote about mystification and misrepresentation to elicit people's interest and respect. An example would be de Gaulle's occasional 'disappearances' to make important decisions. This studied detachment created a sense of respect, and even awe, among many French. Particularly subtly, Guicciardini writes: 'When you have any object in view that you would conceal from others, or would have others believe different from what it is, endeavour to show them by the strongest and gravest reasons you can use that you intend the contrary. For when men imagine you to be convinced that reason favours a particular course, they readily persuade themselves that your resolves will tally with what your reason dictates'.[18]

Human behaviour, however unpredictable, is nevertheless consistent in the creation of events (fortune apart) and is a determining factor in geohistory. Let us now look at the link between individual and corporate/state characteristics.

Connecting

When individuals get together, for whatever reason, whether it be blood, language, faith or, more dangerously, interest, individual habits tend to become customs, which in turn become traditions, all underpinned by characteristics. Many moons ago, it was the shared traditions of tribes, and then groups of tribes, that led naturally to the creation of entities, which by modern times had led to named countries. Borders were obviously the essential way of demonstrating that a people formed an organisational unit with laws. Whether that state/unit was an oligarchy, plutocracy, monarchy, democracy, tyranny et al., or a combination of some or all of these, is not something with which we need concern ourselves here, as our quest is to find the link(s) between individual and corporate/state characteristics.

The older and more established the state, the more entrenched will be the characteristics of its people, since the institutions established hundreds of years ago are part and parcel of those states. Such states (and we are thinking, here for example, of France, England and Japan) have a certain linguistic continuity and an unbroken line of literature going back to even before the state was formed. We do not wish to delve too much into precise characteristics of a people, especially since recent world developments are leading to a blurring of traditional ideas of homogeneity. But, at the risk of sounding trite, we can nevertheless say the English, and the Welsh and Scots to a lesser extent, tend towards insularity in their mentality. History explains why: apart from being an island, England (later the United Kingdom) built up the biggest known empire. As a result, the English language began its march around the world, and the English did not bother, as a rule, to learn other languages. Generally, the English are poor linguists. But their history has made them pragmatists *par excellence*, as reflected in their way of shying away from the abstract, and their tendency towards utilitarian philosophy. Here, it can be argued that this pragmatism comes from the individual, who has a tendency not to commit himself too much, eschewing grandiose ideas requiring commitment. This has translated itself to a national level, particularly regarding Britain's attitude towards European integration, which is more coy and circumspect than that of the French: 'Mr. Schuman and his colleagues were in effect starting with a broad conception, not lacking in nobility and grandeur, requiring a commitment of principle from the outset. This was inimical to British practice and mental habits'.[19]

In contrast to old states, we have the interesting examples of Italy and Germany—interesting, because the geographical descriptions of those two countries are far older than the states themselves. Whether one was in Rome, Florence or Milan in the Middle Ages, the people felt themselves Italian, particularly because of their history and common—at least written—language. Machiavelli wanted a united Italy, his dream coming to fruition over three hundred years later. The same can be said of Germany: history, language and war brought most Germans together in 1871. But when Germany was divided into two states following the last world war, it was to be only two generations before they united again. Thus, we see atavism winning over an unnatural geopolitical division.

These admittedly trite observations can, however, be made reasonably accurate, thanks to our geohistorical prism of the past, which is with us as we write. The same things return: Thatcher's policy on Europe reflected

Bevin's years earlier, while the French mini-revolutions of 1830, 1848 and 1968 were based atavistically speaking on the events of 1789. Trite yet true. If any of you readers start to look at your own countries geohistorically, you will understand matters clearly, without your understanding being invaded by geopolitics and its accompanying pseudo-theoretical and ideological baggage.

Here, geography per se enters the scene: if one considers Germany geohistorically, one sees that this powerful area of Europe has always been surrounded, and felt itself to be surrounded, by hostile, and potentially hostile, neighbours, which in turn partly explains one of the deep causes of the Third and Fourth World Wars, and a subsequent tendency towards the logic of aggression, explained to some extent via geopolitics à la Haushofer.

While it can be tricky and indeed exhausting to attempt to find precise links between individual characteristics and national ones, they exist in the individual and mass consciousness of any reasonably old system, whether a state, church, club or even a business organisation (although the latter do not generally last for hundreds of years), and are a crucial ingredient of understanding geohistory. An individual feels part of his organisation, whether it be a state or a club, and this feeling of belonging and identity, and relationship with the organisation, as well as within the said organisation, whether as a leader or follower, can act as a subliminal point of reference in determining the behaviour emanating from individual characteristics. In Goffman's (see above) 'dramatist' view, organisations are divided broadly into ones of self-interest, where status is not important, and cliques, where members of other groups are kept at bay. Within an organisation, dark secrets are something negative, known only to a few, while inside secrets refer to the whole membership. Guicciardini has the last word, at least in affairs of state: 'It profits much that you conduct your affairs secretly, but much more that you contrive not to seem secret to your friends. For many men, when they see you unwilling to impart your affairs to them, look on it as a slight and feel affronted'.[20]

Conclusions

In this, our foray into explaining geohistory, we can establish that it is the very antithesis of geopolitics, with the latter's emphasis on resources, land-grabbing and its attempt to mix geography with politics. If geohistory becomes the norm, then we are likely to see a reduction in resource-grabbing and war, with little need to promote this or that theory, since learning from history through the hard scrutiny of documents, and the detached thinking that can result, is the basis.

While it may be true that people and groups of people are a product of their geographical environment (climate and location are indeed crucial in the development of peoples), geohistory allows us to look at matters dispassionately without such geopolitics-related terms as 'geostrategy', which is simply a linguistically bulimic term for 'strategy', and often synonymous with 'geokilling'. Geohistory also frees us from using the numerous clashing international relations theories and models; it uses original documents to a large extent, à la Guicciardini. The documents are themselves history. By way of contrast, the likes of Nietzsche, Hegel, Marx and others, despite their rarefied intellectual and occasionally over-logical approach—often based on a pedantic over-interpretation of pre-Socratic, as well as post-Socratic, philosophy—appear to relate their accumulation of facts to their particular concept of history, thereby raising history to an unreal philosophical pedestal, in turn implying by default that history is itself a philosophy, rather than what it really is: the past, which is with us as we write.

Geohistory is not subject to theory. It is per se entirely separate. Some historiographers, in their attempts to put history in a philosophical, or at least theoretical, cage, do little more than stimulate thought processes, but so many, that clashes and disputes occur. Better to use geohistory to understand the way in which the perpetrators of history, mainly humans, think, and how they have influenced many into behaving barbarically, often because the ideas were taken out of context, and even twisted beyond recognition of the original.

History shows us that the same basic characteristics, whether individual, corporate, racial, nationalistic or institutional, tend to remain remarkably constant, modifications notwithstanding, even if they often remain submerged before reasserting themselves. Behaviour itself is consistent in its inconsistency. Geohistory is a tough path to avoid strife where possible, rather than justifying it, as geopolitics often tends to do, with its partner, globalisation, to which we now turn.

NOTES

1. Hill, Christopher, *The Changing Politics of Foreign Policy*, Palgrave Macmillan, Basingstoke, 2003, p. 117.
2. Guicciardini, Francesco, *Counsels and Reflections*, translated from the Italian (*Ricordi Politici e Civili*) by Ninian Hill Thomson, MA, Kegan Paul, Trench Trübner & Co., Ltd., London, 1890, 58, p. 30.
3. Ibid., 1, p. 1.
4. See Vico, Giambattista, *New Science: Principles of the New Science Concerning the Common Nature of Nations*, Penguin Books, London, New York, etc., 1999, reprinted with corrections 2001, taken from the third edition of 1744; translated by David Marsh.
5. Andrew Apostolou, Methoni (Messinia), 17 July 2009, *interview*.
6. I interpret this as 'social animal'.
7. Op. cit., Guicciardini, *Ricordi*, 236, p. 105. Religion should not be confused with faith here. In contrast to his views on the state of the Church, he writes: 'I find no fault with prayer, fasting, and such other devout observances as are either prescribed by the Church or recommended by the Friars. But the best of all good observances, and in comparison wherewith all others are insignificant, is to wrong no man and do what good you can to all' (159, p. 71.).
8. Chairman of the Senate Armed Services Committee, and Republican presidential candidate in 2008.
9. Phillips to Secretary of State, 31 May 1977; *Diplomatic Report* no. 215/77, NA-FCO 9/2669, file WST 014/1, part B, in Mallinson, William, *Thrice a Stranger: Penelope's Easter Mediterranean Odyssey*, Cambridge Scholars Publishing, Newcastle upon Tyne, 2016, p. 71.
10. The Slavs were, however, fully incorporated into the Greek Christian Orthodox way of life.
11. Sutherland to Foreign Secretary, 23 January 1981, *Greece: Annual Review for 1980*, BNA-FCO 9/3175, file WSG 014/2, in Mallinson, William, *Behind the Words: the FCO, Hegemonolingualism and the End of Britain's Freedom*, Cambridge Scholars Publishing, Newcastle upon Tyne, 2014, p. 59.
12. Hence the claim that the inhabitants of North Macedonia are the descendants of the Macedonians.
13. (Secret) *Report on the 'Free Macedonia Movement'*, BNA-FO 371/43649, file R 232,039/1009/67.
14. However, the language used today was nevertheless codified and standardised in the Fifties by Blaze Konevski, who published the first dictionary in 1961.
15. Op. cit., Guicciardini, *Ricordi*, 44, pp. 25, 26.
16. Ibid., 42, p. 25.

17. Goffman, Erving, *The Presentation of Self in Everyday Life*, Penguin, 1984.
18. Op. cit., Guicciardini, *Ricordi*, 199, p. 89.
19. Dilks, David, 'Britain and Europe 1948–1950: The Prime Minister, the Foreign Secretary and the Cabinet', Poidevin, Raymond (ed.), *Histoire des débuts de la Construction Européenne, mars 1948-mai 1950*, Brussels, Milan, Paris, Baden-Baden, 1988.
20. Op. cit., Guicciardini, *Ricordi*, 235, p. 104.

BIBLIOGRAPHY

Dilks, David, 'Britain and Europe 1948–1950: The Prime Minister, the Foreign Secretary and the Cabinet', Poidevin, Raymond (ed.), *Histoire des débuts de la Construction Européenne, mars 1948-mai 1950*, Brussels, Milan, Paris, Baden-Baden, 1988.

Goffman, Erving, *The Presentation of Self in Everyday Life*, Penguin, 1984.

Guicciardini, Francesco, *Counsels and Reflections*, translated from the Italian (*Ricordi Politici e Civili*) by Ninian Hill Thomson, MA, Kegan Paul, Trench Trübner & Co., Ltd., London, 1890.

Hill, Christopher, *The Changing Politics of Foreign Policy*, Palgrave Macmillan, Basingstoke, 2003.

Mallinson, William, *Behind the Words: The FCO, Hegemonolingualism and the End of Britain's Freedom*, Cambridge Scholars Publishing, Newcastle upon Tyne, 2014.

Mallinson, William, *Thrice a Stranger: Penelope's Easter Mediterranean Odyssey*, Cambridge Scholars Publishing, Newcastle upon Tyne, 2016.

Vico, Giambattista, *New Science: Principles of the New Science Concerning the Common Nature of Nations*, Penguin Books, London, New York etc., 1999.

CHAPTER 7

The Effects of Globalisation

Abstract This chapter will explore the connexions between geopolitics and globalisation. Both terms tend to be laden with linguistically bulimic phraseology, such as 'global world'. The effects of globalisation on relations between states within the context of a geopolitical mindset will be considered, given its close connexion to international business. The so-called information explosion will be looked at, given the speed with which people have to move, which naturally detracts from thinking of the implications of their hurriedly, deadline-driven actions. The effect on the British Foreign Commonwealth and Development Office will be considered. Lessons will be drawn from geohistory.

Keywords Globalisation · Geopolitics · Information explosion · Technology · Speed · Diplomacy

What is this life, if, full of care,
We have no time to stand and stare?[1]
William Henry Davies

© The Author(s), under exclusive license to Springer Nature
Switzerland AG 2021
W. Mallinson, *Guicciardini, Geopolitics and Geohistory*,
Palgrave Studies in International Relations,
https://doi.org/10.1007/978-3-030-76537-8_7

Introduction

This chapter will explore the connexions between geopolitics and globalisation. Both terms tend to be laden with linguistically bulimic phraseology, such as 'global world'. The effects of globalisation on inter-state relations within the context of a geopolitical mindset will be considered. Let us first consider the so-called information explosion and its effects.

Information Explosion

The terms 'globalisation' and 'information explosion' appeared within a few years of each other and were presented by international business corporations as new and positive phenomena, even if globalisation, in fact if not in name, began almost five hundred years ago, with Magellan's circumnavigation.

Well before the Internet, the Marshall Plan's slogan 'Prosperity makes you Free'[2] accompanied the further expansion of giant multi-nationals[3] into Western Europe, accompanied in turn by the marketing of American business ideas. Later on, the Internet, and the possibility of instant communication and access to information that would have taken days or even weeks to ascertain, led to a rapid acceleration of the pace at which people lived, with increasingly packed agendas and one deadline after another. Global marketing and communication became the new catchwords, with large multinationals sometimes cleverly disguising their agendas with the phrase 'think local'.[4]

An enormous push came with the so-called Third Way, an attempt by President Clinton and Prime Minister Blair to distract people from the 'extremes' of the two dominant philosophies of the Cold War divide, by using a 'Third Way', a sort of 'New Centre' born of the 'New Left', promoted in Anthony Giddens' book.[5] For many, it appeared as a form of meta-Marxism. But 'Third Way' publicity defined the new approach by what it was not, rather than describing precisely what it was. It contained many references to globalisation, only rarely mentioning the word 'liberty', but used the word 'fraternity'. In this, it can be seen as an attempt to merge politics and business. For Ralph Dahrendorf, it manifested an absence of historical awareness.[6] At any rate, the Third Way, although it has now disappeared, at least in name, nevertheless epitomises the tendency towards global sloganising. The term 'geopolitics' has itself now become a universal term. So much for this brief 'macro-view' of the background. Let us now consider some of the terminology and its effect.

THE END OF MEANING?

Confucius is said to have said that if language is not correct, then what is said is not what is meant, and that if what is said is not what is meant, then what ought to be done remains undone. The language of digital electronic globalisation appears to have adversely affected clarity and understanding. For example, some years ago, when a British Council representative spoke to an audience of students, teachers and business people about the benefits of 'global education',[7] she managed, in the space of only a few minutes, to come up with phrases and expressions such as: 'We all live in a global world', 'intercultural skills', 'global citizenship', 'shared future', 'knowledge workers', 'knowledge creation', 'shared values', 'cutting edge English language', 'education as a force for change' and, of course 'innovation'. This free and automatic use of American— and now English and global—business phraseology seems to now be a *sine qua non* of all budding modern educationalists who see education as a quantifiable and expandable business market, whether public or private. Education has been affected by political and business discourse. Higher Education is now more akin to business training than the hard academic study of cognate disciplines.

The problem is that much of the above global language often lacks intrinsic meaning, even if it can sound sensational and seductive. Yet in this context, globalisation really means homogenisation, since the more uniform the customers, the simpler and cheaper the production, promotion and selling of products worldwide, whether educational or otherwise.

The next step from the seductive phrase 'managing change' is managing, or rather, controlling, thought, as we rush unseeingly into a state of mass intellectual dumbing down, induced not only from outside, but also by our own mental sloth and consequent lack of independent thinking. By using another trendy word, 'empowerment', marketeers have also sold us the idea that we are strong and independent. In fact, we are becoming the opposite. People can even suffer from a form of cognitive self-dissonance and rationalise themselves into believing that they are something which they are not. For example, a man who believes himself to be a gentleman dies trying to rescue a dog. In William Somerset

Maugham's words: 'Like a man who cherishes a vice till it gets a stranglehold on him so that he is its helpless slave, he had lied so long that he had come to believe his own lies. Bob Forrestier had pretended for so many years to be a gentleman that in the end, forgetting that it was all a fake, he had found himself driven to act as, in that stupid, conventional brain of his, he thought a gentleman must act. No longer knowing the difference between sham and real, he had sacrificed his life to a spurious heroism'.[8]

It can be argued that the information explosion and globalisation have enhanced this tendency towards rationalisation, or creating a form of pseudo-reality. Russia's former Prime Minister Dmitry Medvedev hits the nail on the head: 'I am talking about the unprecedented role in public politics of social networks and new media and, accordingly, of private IT companies that own those platforms. […] Isn't it, indeed, a spectre of cyber totalitarianism that is gradually overwhelming society, taking away from it (and potentially the entire world) the opportunity to see reality for what it is?'.[9]

While this is not the place for a deep analysis of the linguistics, semantics and semiotics of the information explosion and globalisation à la de Saussure and Eco, we can pose some pertinent questions about the lack of precision in the language used. What, for example, is a 'knowledge worker'? Is he or she a teacher working in the field of knowledge? Is it someone trying to create knowledge? And if so, on whose terms? And what exactly is 'managing change'? Could it mean 'manipulating events'? For that matter, what is meant by 'change'? Innovation? Substitution? Development? To borrow from, and paraphrase George Orwell slightly, is there not a danger that those who use the above phrases are turning themselves into machines, a result of the hegemonolinguistic terminology of globalisation? The creators of 'shared values'—who do not explain what these values are—by auto-lobotomising themselves into a state of conformity, influence the customers, who can themselves eventually be seduced into automatic acceptance that their values are shared by everybody else.

We ought, however, to qualify this criticism with a quote: 'The Americans […] have invented so wide a range of pithy and hackneyed phrases that they can carry on an amusing and animated conversation without giving a moment's reflection to what they are saying and so leave their minds free to consider the more important matters of big business and fornication'.[10]

Unlike data/information, knowledge cannot be numerically quantified. As we have intimated, putting human affairs into exact formulae shows a lack of wisdom. In other words, you cannot catch the human mind, on which the very existence of knowledge depends. It is quite possible that, bored with the bromide 'knowledge management', the slogan-sellers will soon start using the catchphrase 'wisdom management'. Dead fish swim with the current.

In short, independence of thought is flushed away, while redundant shibboleths rule the pseudo-linguistic roost. In the end, the inappropriate use of technology actually means that communication is destroying communication, ironically in the name of communication. The answer is to forget the obsession with 'going forward', and to sometimes go backwards, by bringing back the basics, such as good grammar, clarity of expression and reading skills. If one looks at British examination papers from the Sixties set for the Common Entrance for public (independent) schools, taken by twelve- and thirteen-year-old pupils, they are equivalent in standard to something between today's British GCSE and A Levels, generally taken by sixteen- to eighteen-year-olds. Today's youth appears to be less educated than in past years, despite (or because of?) the digital globalisation engendered by the misuse of the information explosion and its accompanying technology. A few years ago, a Vatican ambassador to Britain described technology as a morally neutral tool that had served the Church well, but added that its use could be dangerous. For example, a hammer could be used to fashion beautiful wrought iron, but also to break skulls.[11]

There seems to be an automatic assumption that technological progress is positive and civilised, when it is in fact often exploited without regard for its long-term effects. To put it bluntly, there is no proof that technological gadgets or the neutron bomb has made humanity more civilised, unless killing people more efficiently and in ever greater numbers is progress. Giving cannibals knives and forks may be done in the name of progress; but this progress may simply make them eat other humans more efficiently, and just as greedily. In this connexion, the Smartphone, if misused, can change opinions into 'appinions' and be a substitute for thinking. To put it dramatically, if rather strongly, 'a zombie apocalypse' comes to mind. Smartphones, or rather the plethora of 'apps', can also contribute to the trivialisation of serious issues. A quote by a virologist shows the dangers of Twitter generally in creating stress and bedevilling efficiency: 'Trying to defend myself on Twitter against attacks: that never works. In general, I made the mistake of spending too much time reading Twitter. Doing so just drives you crazy. And then, it was naïve of me to just announce in brief on Twitter the results of our study on viral load in children. Many people saw that as a provocation'.[12]

Despite the claim that the information revolution/explosion has raised the level of public intelligence, the opposite seems to be becoming the case, with people's (especially youths') knowledge of general knowledge diminishing.[13] This has affected, for example, British policy formulators. *The Spectator* sets the tone: 'A friend of mine has just come back from a few days of Civil Service inhouse training. He managed in no time to get the hang of the exercise. Namely, the mastery of another language. Not a foreign language, which might have been handy, but not English either. 'I learnt', he said proudly, 'about "brain-friendly learning", "career pathing", "energy management" and – my absolute favourite – "impact residue", which is what you leave behind when you have met someone: what the uninitiated would call a lasting impression. I was encouraged to "flex my styles" and identify "meta-objectives". In short, I am a new man'. In other words, he's learned management-speak [...] I came across a little booklet issued by the Foreign and Commonwealth Office for the use of its staff. It was a fine example of the genre. It was called *Stakeholder Engagement*, and it came with the imprimatur of Peter Ricketts, the department's permanent under-secretary, and David Milliband, then the foreign secretary. Under the new government, the Stakeholder Engagement Team which generated it is going strong and there is, for good measure, a 'network of stakeholder managers'. The introduction set the tone.

'Stakeholder management', it declared, 'is the core of diplomacy and service delivery'. We have engaged many of our stakeholders in the development and delivery of our objectives. We must continue to do this across the board in a strategic, systematic and innovative manner. It doesn't actually say what a stakeholder is. Just that his management is the core of 'service delivery'. Four paragraphs down, we do get a definition of a stakeholder, as 'those organisations and individuals who can affect the achievement of FCO's objectives...we must engage with...stakeholders that have most potential influence'. I showed it to a friend who used to work in the Foreign Office and he said tersely: 'It means we should be talking to, when and how''.[14]

Another example of global business language's invasion of the public sector comes to mind: 'Maintenance and development of the UK narrative around FCO and its value proposition, using insights from research and evaluation as well as knowledge of the evolving FCO strategy to inform resonant messaging'.[15] In plain Standard English, this simply means 'working out improved ways of informing people about the FCO's work'.

Various catchphrases are now used liberally by civil servants and politicians alike. In the words of one, 'going forward' has infected the world of diplomacy just as thoroughly as the world of business, as has talk of 'stakeholders'.[16] Here, T.S. Eliot comes to mind: 'Where is the wisdom lost to knowledge, where is the knowledge lost to information and where is the word we lost in words?'.

Technology, Speed and Greed

An old Italian proverb, little heeded in the world of globalisation, runs: 'He who goes slowly goes healthily and far'. It is often accompanied by 'He who goes fast goes to his death'.[17] Perhaps the most ignored phenomenon of geopolitics within the framework of the digital information explosion and globalisation is speed. Guicciardini explains: 'The very same things which, when undertaken at the proper moment, readily succeed, and, so to speak, accomplish themselves, will, if tempted prematurely, not merely fail then, but will often also lose their aptitude for succeeding at their own time. Accordingly, you are not to rush hastily on any enterprise, nor to precipitate events, but to await their season and maturity'.[18]

Since the advent of the Industrial Revolution, Mankind has been trying to move ever faster. This is not to say that speed was not an objective of early civilisations. The Greeks, for example, with their development of ever faster ships, were able to conquer and to trade more effectively, while the Romans improved their military power through building roads to transport troops and chariots at ever increasing speed. It is, however, the increasing pace of living itself which has characterised developments since the Industrial Revolution. Travel became ever faster with the building of canals and new types of road surfacing, and then the invention of the aeroplane. Mass production meant that quotas and deadlines had to be achieved. The masses began to be seen by the rich élites as human machines. However negative and politically incorrect it may sound to the 'snowflake-minded', let us quote Lady Chatterley's husband, back in the Twenties: 'The masses were always the same, and will always be the same. Nero's slaves were extremely little different from our colliers or the Ford motor-car workmen. I mean Nero's mine slaves and his field slaves. It is the masses: they are unchangeable. An individual may emerge from the masses. But the emergence doesn't alter the mass. The masses are unalterable. It is one of the most momentous facts of social science. *Panem et circenses!*'.[19]

Today, we praise ourselves on no longer thinking like Lady Chatterley's husband. But, to extrapolate from Guicciardini, perhaps things are not so very different in terms of basic human characteristics, but persist in new colours and with new names. As the primary and secondary sectors have shrunk in favour of the tertiary, it can be argued that the masses are been led into digitalisation, owing to the predominance of huge information technology corporations acting globally and controlling electronic communications. IT corporations are buying into energy companies and exerting their digital influence over the whole US military-industrial-congressional complex, thereby increasing their power over people. If power corrupts, then absolute power corrupts absolutely, and there is a danger of absolutism. Elon Musk has said that autonomous machines are more dangerous to the world than North Korea and could unleash 'weapons of terror'. He has compared the adoption of AI to 'summoning the devil'.[20]

President Putin is also worried: on the one hand, he points out that machines, even if they can perform a task better than a human (viz. an excavator), do not think. Yet he also says that whichever country manages to perfect AI will rule the world. His concern is that humanity needs to control AI, and not the other way round, adding that 'like any artificial thing, an artificial intelligence has no heart, no soul, no feeling of compassion, no conscience'.[21] More scathingly, he said a month later: 'Where is the line between a successful global business, in-demand services and consolidation of big data – and attempts to harshly and unilaterally govern society, replace legitimate democratic institutions, restrict one's natural right to decide for themselves how to live, what to choose, what stance to express freely? We've all seen this just now in the US. And everybody understands what I'm talking about'.[22]

A certain measure of chaos and confusion is palpable today: traditional jobs are being lost, and those unable to cope with digitalisation are falling by the wayside. Airport digital booking systems are crashing, despite the 'progress' of AI. Military systems are threatened by all manner of cyber warfare, which could possibly lead to a nuclear button being activated by a mad president, because the 'intelligent' computer has not been properly fed with the correct applications. Our so-called emerging (another catchword of globalisation) technologies—including the mobile Internet, autonomous vehicles and advanced genomics—are already beginning to cause confusion, mainly because it seems almost impossible to define what the impact on the life we lead will be. We can of course already say that various so-called apps are replacing natural face-to-face communication, as well as writing and reading skills. Here, of course, we have a double-edged sword: on the one hand, some form of control is needed to prevent a mad spiral leading to self-assured mutual destruction, while on the other, that control can, in the wrong hands, lead to enslavement of the human race by a small group of power-seekers. Although the second option is surely better than the end of humanity, a Guicciardinian approach would entail the seeking of a happy medium, seek ways to slow down, and eliminate exaggerated greed and speed.

It can be argued that a new form of totalitarianism is developing by stealth, rather than through latter-day Fascism, Nazism or Bolshevism. People are becoming so dependent on digitalisation that they almost welcome being controlled, while believing that they are 'empowered'. But for some others, matters can be grimmer: in both private and working lives, people are obliged to have a computer and the Internet to access bank accounts, since local branches are closing down. Gone are the days when most people could directly telephone a tax inspector or bank clerk, let alone have a friendly chat with a bank manager. It can even be difficult to buy a rail ticket without a Smartphone. To talk to someone on the telephone, one has to wait for up to an hour, pressing various buttons and listening to music. In the face of globalisation, small retailers are closing down, leaving consumers with no choice but to be 'empowered' into having to buy from the titans.

In this connexion, we turn to the so-called Great Reset. Those who criticise its implications tend to be labelled as 'conspiracy theorists'. Their critique runs something like this: 'Imagine a world controlled by a small group of people with the extreme power to control the flow of goods, services and other resources around the world. They have the ability to dictate to governments around the world to impose certain health mandates. They have the power to require passes for travel, and to have people confined to their homes. They have the power to tell retailers to refuse cash. This small group of people control the networks of commerce. One has only to consider the power of Amazon and Google (to name but a few) to realise the danger to individual freedom posed by these concentrated financial interests. Klaus Schwab, founder of the World Economic Forum, is even using Prince Charles as his useful PR idiot'.

The question must be posed as to how seriously the Schwabs of this world—and their followers—should be taken. That financial power is becoming increasingly concentrated in the hands of less people is hardly open to dispute. But it does not necessarily mean, as Schwab claims, that somehow governments will agree, and act on, a 'Great Reset', or the 'Fourth Industrial Revolution', as Schwab terms it. In some ways, he and those of his ilk have jumped onto a bandwagon, praising, for example, the increasing tendency away from cash payments, and forcing people to buy Smartphones to pay for certain things, which depend on various 'apps'. These developments were with us well before Schwab's 'Great Reset' was announced.

Some serious people have criticised the ideas contained in the 'Great Reset', even some in the much criticised 'mainstream media'. For example, on 15 November 2020, Sky News Australia presenter Rowan Dean stated: 'It is a global commitment they have made to use the panic and fear generated by the corona virus as a means to reshape all our economies and laws and move to a new form of capitalism that focusses on net zero emissions, to use all the tools of COVID to tackle climate change. If implemented successfully, The Great Reset will undeniably and deliberately have extreme and possibly dire repercussions. "You'll own nothing, and you'll be happy" is just one of their marketing slogans. The plan involves replacing shareholders of big companies with stakeholders, who happen to be left-wing bureaucrats and climate change zealots. Replacing Mum and Dad's small businesses and private enterprises with big tech and big business. Remember, it's not only a great reset, it's a great deception'.[23]

Even Fox News has weighed in, through its presenter and journalist Carlson Tucker, who wrote: 'The most intimate details of our lives are being completely controlled by our leadership class. The people who used to scream at politicians, "Keep your hands off my body!" aren't saying a thing about this. In fact, they're encouraging it. So the question is, what exactly is this about? It's not about science. If masks and lockdowns prevented spikes in coronavirus infections, we wouldn't be seeing spikes in coronavirus infections after nine months. But we are seeing them, so clearly, the geniuses got it wrong once again. This time, they're not even bothering to point to legitimate scientific studies to support continuing their policies because there aren't any studies that support that. So what is going on?'.[24]

The owner of a large British-based international design company is scathing about how digitalisation is being abused: 'The power-mongers' message of individual 'empowerment' is utterly hypocritical, since it is merely the semantic seduction of individuality, leading to slavery, and control by the few. The more uniform the customers, the simpler and cheaper the production, promotion and selling of goods, thus leading to a lack of quality and creativity. [...] Information, or rather the control of it, is power. And somewhere, behind all this, lurks the idea that the military-industrial-congressional complex is pulling the strings. All very paranoid, you might think, but remember that plotters do their utmost to dismiss critics as conspiracy theorists'.[25]

It can be said that the rush towards digitalisation of our lives is leading to an imbalance between big (private) business and government, with the private sector gaining in influence. Although the public and private sectors have been ingredients of governments for centuries, recent developments suggest that global businesses—or, rather, billionaire shareholders—are beginning to exert an unhealthy influence on government policies. Globalisation has encouraged giant corporations to coordinate their policies ever more tightly. We can refer to the Trilateral Commission, set up in 1973 to study relations between Japan, the US and Western Europe, and to propose policies for economic, political and defence relations between the three.[26] This can be seen as marking the beginning of an attempt to merge the public and private interests of the democratic and capitalist West across the globe. An FCO official minuted 'Who pays?' on an explanatory document. The answer was David Rockefeller and big business. When in 1999 I asked the former British Foreign Secretary, David Owen, who was paying for his invitation to Athens (to convince Greeks, *inter alia*, that it had been necessary to bomb Serbia), he answered that it was the Trilateral Commission.[27] I told him that I had never heard of it, whereupon he said that it was Rockefeller. At the time, the Trilateral Commission was considered by some to be the world's most powerful coalition of governing élites.[28] It still exists today, but is less in the public eye than its slightly older homologue, the World Economic Forum, which is 'committed to improving the state of the world by engaging business, political, academic, and other leaders of society to shape global, regional, and industry agendas'.²⁹

While these organisations were—laudably—set up to promote world peace, the agenda has altered, as we have seen from some of the criticisms above. The financial clout of the information technology industry, or rather of its shareholders, is leading to increasing commercialisation of the public sector, with the language of geopolitics, globalisation and digitalisation merging into a quest to control resources at a global level. Guicciardini puts a pertinent slant on this: 'For greedy men believe easily whatsoever they desire, and simple men know not when they are deceived'.³⁰ Thus, a critic of Schwab's 'Great Reset' might say that the rich are deceiving the masses. Yet more pertinently, according to Guicciardini, 'the Duke of Ferrara, who occupies himself with trade, with monopolies, and such other vulgar pursuits as are fit only for private men to engage in, merits the severest blame'.³¹ This quotation truly encapsulates the danger of business taking over governments or at least dictating policy.

Technology is encouraging speed, which is in turn engendering more greed. This is particularly evident in the world of finance. An English language teacher sums it up well: 'I coach some very senior types in France's biggest banking groups and 'Fintech'³² is a hot topic indeed during all my sessions. In fact, the big banks are running scared and being forced to adapt their strategies because of these start-ups (another buzzword) which, as you probably know, offer innovative (not to be confused with creative or original), ways of carrying out financial transactions using the latest technology (cutting edge…). The answer for some banks is to buy the Fintechs! Really just another stage in what is currently referred to in France as the 'Uberisation' of society. 'Chief Digital Officer' is the latest job title being bandied about in the banking sphere. What with the accumulating mass of regulations from the European Central Bank (all in English), no wonder my students are often on sick leave, in the middle of divorces, have serious conflicts with colleagues or just come across as half-asleep most of the time'.

The Attack on Diplomacy

Professional diplomats are the nuts and bolts of relations between states. Before electronic communication came to the fore, they had considerable authority, but once political leaders in different countries could communicate with each other on the telephone, jump on an aeroplane to meet their homologues abroad and nowadays hold video conferences, ambassadors and their staff and officials at home found their importance diminishing to that of a public relations agent. Nevertheless, their advisory rôle remained crucial: a foreign minister can hardly be expected to know his counterparts the world over, let alone the hundreds of bilateral issues between his country and the two hundred odd countries with which his country has relations.

Globalisation and the speed of its accompanying digital technology have had a major effect on traditional diplomacy. Although we do not have the space to research, analyse and evaluate how technology has affected diplomatic services worldwide, the case of the British Foreign, Commonwealth and Development Office (FCDO) can be considered.[33]

First, some history: the 'engine room' of a department was the 'Third Room', after the head of department's and the assistant head of department's offices, respectively. Here, desk officers drafted replies to parliamentary questions, wrote briefs for delegations, answered queries from ministers, drafted and answered telegrams, exchanged minutes with other members of the department or desk officers in other departments and replied to letters from members of the public, usually on a minister's behalf. Then, there were policy meetings, as well as regular departmental ones, known as 'morning prayers'. Whenever a minister sought advice, the first thing a desk officer did was to check British policy on the question that the minister wanted to be answered, by calling for the file from the registry, the latter being a veritable library of all the work done by the department, a written collective memory. Having formed a picture, the desk officer would then submit a draft answer via his out tray to the assistant head of department, who would then amend the text by hand, show the desk officer the alterations and submit it to the head of department, who would if necessary add his handwritten amendments. If the draft were to end up as a letter, policy statement or answer to a written parliamentary question by a minister, it would wend its way further up the tree to the relevant Assistant Under-Secretary, and perhaps to an Under-Secretary, before being submitted to the minister for signature. If it involved a particularly important or sensitive matter, it might even be submitted to the Permanent Under-Secretary himself. The desk officer was able to see how his written work had improved on the way to the top. Only minutes were not checked, perhaps understandably, since they were initiated and signed by the desk officer. There were three ways of producing written work: by hand, then passing it to the typing pool;

dictating to a shorthand typist; or dictating into a machine, to be handed to the typist. Staff had the mental space to reflect on their work.

Now things are very different. The registry no longer exists, the typing pools have disappeared and ambassadors no longer write valedictory despatches. Despatches as a whole are disappearing. With the slow but inexorable introduction of the desktop computer, e-grams (the first one was sent in 2004) have replaced telegrams, and minutes are e-mailed to colleagues, sometimes in the same room. Since there are no registries, it is far more difficult to access the file: instead, there is a series of cumbersome electronic steps to be gone through. Although all communications are meant to be registered, the procedure is far too time-consuming for most officers to bother to register a minute, letter or e-gram. In the serious days, whenever one read a letter, telegram or report, and had acted on it, one wrote either 'pa' ('put away') or 'BU' ('Bring Up') with a date. Before filing the paper, the registry clerk would note the 'BU' date and give the file to the desk officer on the desired date. All that is gone. According to a recently retired ambassador,[34] the collective memory has gone, and most written work is done 'on the hoof'. Where once the FCO had three personnel departments, namely Personnel Operations Department, Personnel Services Department and Personnel Policy Department, there is now a 'Human Resources Directorate'. Where there was once Training Department, we now have the same Human Resources Directorate, which includes a 'Recruitment and Development Department', including in turn a 'Learning and Development Team'.

As we have seen, the FCOD now uses the language of globalisation. This change has been accompanied by a dumbing down in training. A human resource (person) no longer benefits from week-long—and longer—drafting courses, which were once run by retired diplomats. They are now offered through 'Civil Service Learning'. Thus, much of the FCO's past expertise in training has been subsumed into the broader Civil Service and partly stultified.

The upshot of all this is that diplomats meet each other far less during their working day, huddled as they are in front of their computers. On-line meetings also often replace face-to-face ones. Electronic communication substitutes for natural communication. The American spell-check, based on American operating systems and *Windows,* has by and large replaced the draft wending its way upwards to be perfected. There is far less formality. Only older members of the service sign letters to their homologues with 'Yours ever', as was once the accepted custom. As for the enjoyable quick gossip sessions, the demise of the registry has killed them off.

It is, however, not fair to blame only younger diplomats: just as parents can be considered responsible for their children's misdemeanours, so are senior diplomats for the vagaries of their younger colleagues. The March 2014 edition of the FCO Association's *Password Magazine*[35] features an interview with the Chief Operating Officer, Matthew Rycroft. The position that he fills was once known as that of 'Chief Clerk', responsible for the FCO's administration and setting an example to younger colleagues. Herewith some extracts of the written interview: 'The culture has changed. We are less hierarchical, more open to the outside, creative and confident. We no longer have a large central HR function working out what is best for each individual and posting them there whatever their personal preferences. Instead, each individual needs to take responsibility for their own career. This approach, much closer to a free market, combined with the introduction of Assessment and Development Centres for key promotion points, has transformed the culture to put much greater emphasis on leadership and management skills. The pendulum is swinging back a bit at the moment, with renewed emphasis on expertise and skills. We need to keep the organisation up to date and adjust regularly. Working practices have changed. IT has transformed how, where and when we work and has prompted a dramatic shift from paper to electronic communication. Flexible working is now embedded into the culture of the organisation. Personally, I work from home in my current role most Fridays, and use the train journeys to work on my Restricted blackberry which is synched to my desktop and laptop. Digital tools have transformed our external engagement—how we get our views across and how we listen to others. We have an extensive digital presence—including 200 country sites—in over 30 languages; 6 Ministers and 80 Ambassadors are on Twitter [...] Our work is now more tightly focussed on our priorities, which are more clearly articulated than used to be the case. We are gradually moving away from traditional 'desk officer' roles covering one topic or region towards more flexible staffing and a project-based approach to policy delivery. Our buildings have changed too. In the UK, we are moving—more slowly than most Government Departments—towards an 8 to 10 ratio of desks to people, with more hot desking to make maximum use of our space [....] We are working hard to achieve 'Diplomatic Excellence', our reform and improvement agenda, with the ambition of being the best Diplomatic Service in the world by 2015 [...] Our vision for

2015 is that the FCO will be an ambitious, confident and creative organisation, highly rated for its policy analysis and action-orientated delivery [...]. In general, careers are more fluid than they used to be, and we need to make it easier for people to come and go. The world is changing very fast, and people's expectations and aspirations are also changing. Not all those joining today will wish to stay with us for their entire career. But for those that do, plenty of opportunities exist to carve out a challenging, rewarding and interesting career. [...] I recognise that this [*esprit de corps*] is one area on which retired staff often say that things aren't the same now as in their day. And it's also an issue that is affected by the economic climate. So let me try to describe aspects of the *esprit de corps* that I feel and see around the globe today. In last year's staff survey, our overall 'engagement' score, based on five questions showing how positive, attached and motivated our staff feel, rose to 68%. It was 10 points above the Civil Service average. So I think staff do generally feel motivated and proud to work for the FCO, despite the pressures that austerity and an ever increasing workload have placed on us all'.[36]

Rycroft proudly tells us that six ministers and eighty ambassadors are on Twitter, almost as if this is the be-all and end-all of successful diplomacy and communication. Yet it is well known how controversial Twitter can be, and that it can lead to all kind of spats, not to mention being open to attack from virtually any quarter. Twitter is essentially a private game, often for people to bloat their egos. Those who use it to promote their official views or careers open themselves to unwarranted attacks from cranks and enemies. To imply that it is a useful part of diplomacy is off-beam. It can actually lead to a dissipation of seriousness and is but a cheap substitute for serious analysis and evaluation, so vital to the formulation of policy. For even if there is still some traditional formulation of policy, it is surely being eroded subliminally in the minds of those responsible for the interests of the United Kingdom. Here, Guicciardini again comes to mind, even if only indirectly: 'Any man who takes upon him to introduce changes into the government of Florence, unless he be constrained thereto by necessity or happen to be at the head of affairs, lacks wisdom. [...] after the change is made you are condemned to endless torment in having always to fear further innovation'.[37] The point here is to show how fashionable innovations can create their own momentum and get out of control.

Conclusions

We have tried to show the effect of globalisation and its accompanying technology on relations between states, within the context of a geopolitical mentality. The recent promotion of globalisation and new electronic technologies occurred at the same time as the promotion of geopolitics in the study and practice of international relations. A common denominator is the alleged breakdown of borders and therefore of national consciousness through bromides such as 'shared values', 'going forward', 'shoulder to shoulder' and the like. Such sloganising suits the geopolitical acquisition of resources such as oil, regardless of international law, as we have seen; it also suits the pioneers of global marketing. Another connexion is the categorisation of people across borders, for example the LGBTQ movement. Paradoxically, by highlighting people's differences in the name of equality, a form of apartheid is created, with an increase in social tensions between and within newly categorised groups. Positive discrimination has also increased with globalisation, creating irritation among, for example, non-Blacks, who feel that they are themselves being discriminated against. The combination of a 'world without borders' and the increasing political power of the large IT corporations, with their 'managing' of individual freedom, is paradoxically leading to an increase in nationalism and even tribalism, as people seek an identity (more about identity in our final chapter). The 'America First' mantra is one example, while the Brexit vote can be seen as another, given the amount of emotion in the debate. The common sense of the 'good fences make good neighbours' idea seems to be less relevant.

The late historian Christopher Lasch looks as if he felt as early as 1995 much of what I am arguing. He puts the malaise better than I can: 'The world of the late twentieth century presents a curious spectacle. On the one hand, it is now united, through the agency of the market, as it never was before. Capital and labor flow freely across political boundaries that seem increasingly artificial and unenforceable. Popular culture follows in their wake. On the other hand, tribal loyalties have seldom been so aggressively promoted. Religious and ethnic warfare breaks out in one country after another [...] It is the weakening of the nation state that underlies both these developments – the movement toward unification and the seemingly contradictory movement toward fragmentation'.[38]

Since then, technology has forced yet more speed on people, and the geopolitical world is becoming increasingly disorganised. Just as a geopolitical mentality was a prime ingredient of the last world war, so it is today, as the attack on Iraq demonstrates so well. In short, it is fair to say that a combination of globalisation and geopolitics is leading to a dangerous spiral into the unknown, leading to a feeling of increasing individual and corporate (state and national) insecurity, and thus totalitarian tendencies and preparation for war. The faster we move, the shorter become our memories, with which we begin our final chapter.

NOTES

1. Mallinson, William, *Images in Words*, Cambridge Scholars Publishing, Newcastle upon Tyne, 2018, 2019.
2. Carruthers, Susan L., 'Not Like Us? Europeans and the Spread of American Culture', *International Affairs*, vol. 74, no. 4, London, October 1998.
3. Although these companies operate in many countries, most of their owners are usually based in one country.
4. For example, the International Telephone and Telegraph corporation (ITT) in the Eighties and Nineties.
5. Giddens, Anthony, *The Third Way: The Renewal of Social Democracy*, Wiley, 1998.
6. Dahrendorf, Ralph, 'The Third Way and Liberty: An Authoritarian Streak in Europe's New Centre', *Foreign Affairs*, vol. 78, no. 5, New York, September/October 1999.
7. Sixth International GUIDE (Global Universities in Distance Education) Conference, Athens, 3 and 4 October 2013.
8. Maugham, W. Somerset, *Collected Short Stories*, Vol. 1, Penguin Books, Harmondsworth, 1970(1st edn., 1951, William Heinemann), p. 283.
9. Medvedev, Dmitry, 'America 2.0. after the Election', *TASS*, 16 January 2021.
10. Maugham, Somerset William, *Cakes and Ale*, Vintage Books, London, 2000, p. 23. First published by William Heinemann in 1930.
11. Barbarito, Archbishop Luigi, London, 3 July 1991, *interview*.
12. *Interview* with virologist Christian Drosten, *Der Spiegel*, 22 January 2021.
13. See Lasch, Christopher, *The Revolt of the Elites*, W.W. Norton & Company, New York and London, 1995, p. 162.
14. McDonagh, Melanie, 'Sir Humphrey's new suit', *The Spectator*, 22 January 2011.
15. Hough, Andrew, 'Foreign Office second language is gibberish, says Plain English Campaign', *Daily Telegraph*, 10 December 2010.

16. Bagehot, *The Economist*, 27 January 2011.
17. Chi va piano va sano e lontano; chi va veloce va incontro alla croce.
18. Op. cit., Guicciardini, *Ricordi*, 78, p. 38.
19. Lawrence, D.H., *Lady Chatterley's Lover*, Penguin Books Ltd., 1960, p. 190.
20. Holley, Peter, 'Elon Musk's Nightmarish Warning: "AI could become "an immortal dictator from which we would never escape"', *Washington Post*, 6 April 2018. Musk is one of the world's richest high-tech entrepreneurs.
21. 'Artificial intelligence for president? I hope not, says Putin, after digital assistant Athena enquires about having his job', *Russia Today, article*, 4 December 2020.
22. *Russia Today*, 27 January 2022, *article*.
23. *Sky News Australia*, 15 November 2021.
24. Carlson Tucker, *Fox News*, 16 November 2020.
25. Minale, Marcello, in an as yet unpublished book on the design industry.
26. See BNA FCO 82/277, file AMU 2/4.
27. Interview with David Owen, Athens, 22 October 1999.
28. *The Athens News* of 22 October 1999 quotes from Peter C. Newman's book, *Titans*.
29. World Economic Forum 'mission statement'.
30. Guicciardini, Francesco, *Counsels and Reflections*, translated from the Italian (*Ricordi Politici e Civili*) by Ninian Hill Thomson, M.A., Kegan Paul, Trench Trübner & Co., Ltd., London, 1890, 105, p. 48.
31. Ibid., 93, p. 43.
32. Financial technology seeking to improve and automate the delivery and use of financial services. It now includes different sectors and industries such as education, retail banking, fundraising and nonprofit, and investment management, to name but some.
33. The FCO was merged with the Department for International Development at the end of 2020.
34. Bill Patey.
35. Recently re-named '*Inside Out*'.
36. Extract of interview from *Password* (the FCO Association magazine), issue 38, March 2014.
37. Op. cit., Guicciardini, *Ricordi*, 51, pp. 27–8.
38. Op. cit., Lasch, pp. 47–8.

Bibliography

Carruthers, Susan L., 'Not Like Us? Europeans and the Spread of American Culture', *International Affairs*, vol. 74, no. 4, London, October 1998.

Dahrendorf, Ralph, 'The Third Way and Liberty: An Authoritarian Streak in Europe's New Centre', *Foreign Affairs*, vol. 78, no. 5, New York, September/October 1999.

Giddens, Anthony, *The Third Way: The Renewal of Social Democracy*, Wiley, 1998.

Guicciardini, Francesco, *Counsels and Reflections*, translated from the Italian (Ricordi Politici e Civili) by Ninian Hill Thomson, M.A., Kegan Paul, Trench Trübner & Co., Ltd., London, 1890.

Lasch, Christopher, *The Revolt of the Elites*, W.W. Norton & Company, New York and London, 1995.

Lawrence, D.H., *Lady Chatterley's Lover*, Penguin Books Ltd., 1960.

Mallinson, William, *Images in Words*, Cambridge Scholars Publishing, Newcastle upon Tyne, 2018, 2019.

Maugham, W. Somerset, (1970), *Collected Short Stories*, Vol. 1, Penguin Books, Harmondsworth (1st edn., 1951, William Heinemann).

Maugham, Somerset William, *Cakes and Ale*, Vintage Books, London, 2000, p. 23. First published by William Heinemann in 1930.

CHAPTER 8

The Ricordi and Memory

Abstract This chapter will tie up all the converging strands of the book into a coherent and cogent whole, using various extracts from Guicciardini's *Ricordi*, but also some of Christopher Hill's ideas, arguing that they tend towards geohistory. Factors such as memory, atavism, nostalgia, nationalism and pride are identified as important in understanding state, as well as individual, behaviour, while reliance on the idea of national interests alone as the key determinant in inter-state relations is accepted too readily and uncritically, particularly given the woolliness of the concept of the nation-state. The significance of scrutinising documents to understand inter-state relations is emphasised.

Keywords Christopher Hill · Memory · Atavism · State behaviour · Nationalism

Nothing is, but thinking makes it so.[1]
Epictetus

INTRODUCTION

This final chapter is intended to tie together the various connected strands about which you have read into a coherent, consistent, cogent and simple

© The Author(s), under exclusive license to Springer Nature Switzerland AG 2021
W. Mallinson, *Guicciardini, Geopolitics and Geohistory*,
Palgrave Studies in International Relations,
https://doi.org/10.1007/978-3-030-76537-8_8

119

whole, ending with some advice from Guicciardini. Let us repeat (see Chapter 1) that this book aims to demonstrate that geohistory, as opposed to geopolitics, is a vital concept in understanding relations between states, at a time of considerable confusion in world affairs, and that Guicciardini's *Ricordi* is an efficient medium to demonstrate not only the inadequacies of geopolitics, but that geohistory should be a more responsible approach to understanding international affairs.

Geohistory diverges strongly from the assumption that relations between states are based exclusively on the elusive balance of power and on state (often disguised as national) interests, neither being easy to define with precision, being broad brush, involving more wood than trees, ignoring the branches, twigs, buds and flowers. The assumption can nevertheless at least serve as a starting point for debate, hence this book.

The question must be posed: is there a definable international system, or merely around two hundred states somehow co-existing, with periods of war and peace, while the world, or parts of it, moves from periods of chaos to order, and back again, as Vico wrote? An answer could be that a state is a system, having developed by default, as an anti-dote to complete disorganisation, leaving around two hundred co-existing systems to treat with each other, creating systems of competing alliances, since there can be no single system unless the world unites into a single state. This is how a geohistorian can begin to understand relations between states, considering, perhaps, Guicciardini's preference for playing off one state against the other. Vico also comes in handy here: 'For whenever nations emerge from their savage, ferocious, and brutish ages, and are civilised by religion, they begin, develop, and end in the same stages'.[2] We shall develop this theme later in this final chapter.

We have considered Guicciardini, the world of international relations theory, geopolitics, the concept of geohistory, globalisation and technology, and concluded that speed, or perhaps to put it better, the sheer pace of events and the speed at which people work, is adding to the greed born of insecurity, leading to a certain lack of common sense and serious reflection in inter-state relations. Before considering how and why a geohistorical approach can slow down and possibly even reverse the threat of war, let us begin by considering history and memory as a path towards describing and explaining the mental underpinning of this book, with no need to limit ourselves to a 'conceptual framework'.

History and Memory

As far as geohistory is concerned, we have said that history is another word for the past, for what has happened. In their purest form, the two words are synonymous. History lies in our memories, which are also filters made up of our own experiences, feelings, loves, hates, fears and prejudices. As such, our knowledge and interpretation of history are held hostage to our human condition, but not to history (the past) itself, since geohistory sets out to separate our own interpreted memory from what has in reality happened, a tough task, since it depends on complete academic detachment. It follows that any interpretation of events should only be questioned on the basis of forensic factuality, rather than of any political agenda, prejudice or personal morality and emotion that people may wish to infer. Hence the importance of the hard scrutiny of documents, which we shall discuss in the following section.

In our contention above, it also follows that we are bipedic memories, only aware of our existence and of what we see because of our memory which, in line with geohistory, is what we term the 'present'. The 'present' cannot stop, as everything moves in perpetuity, with our awareness permanently becoming the past. In this sense, the 'present' is the immediate past. As for the future, that can only be in our minds, in the form of imagination, representing only what we think, want, hope and assume will occur. This opens the door to why Guicciardini attaches such importance to fortune and unpredictability. If this mode of thinking strikes a reader as too outré, then consider people's natural disinclination to walk around in the nude. Expressing to the world one's depth of thinking is also akin to mental nudity, a form of mental striptease. It requires considerable intellectual power and braveness, usually only found in certain great poets, artists and philosophers.

It is hardly surprising that politicians often fear historians, seeing them as detectives. In the words of a historian *par excellence*, 'A historian must not hesitate, even if his books lend aid and comfort to the Queen's enemies […], or even to the common enemies of mankind'.[3] In line with geohistory, the historian has to identify immutable human characteristics and the sometimes varying and vacillating behaviour emanating from them, in order to better locate the facts (perhaps 'facts' is a less emotionally laden word than 'truth'). He has therefore to detach his own prejudices from his research and interpretation of the events that he discovers. This is a hard task. According to Christopher Hill, 'History provides politicians with a welcome form of structure amidst uncertainty, as well as a way of mobilising public opinion behind the government. As individuals, they have personal memories, as representatives of a political class they inherit certain dominant myths, rituals and pieces of conventional thinking which they use and abuse but are also themselves trapped within'.[4] Here, let us hark back to Chapter 3, where I touched on Procrustean models and the tendency to rationalise. Politicians apart, social scientists do not escape Hill's keen eye: 'Social scientists in particular spend their lives analysing history and seeking to discern patterns in it. Those who literally have no sense of the past are amnesiac and as severely disabled as it is possible to be. [...] The need is to look on history not as a store cupboard of the off-the-shelf possible solutions, but as something integral to ourselves and our sense of identity in both time and space. If history is looked upon as perpetual flux, with familiar objects bobbing up regularly in the stream of change, the present becomes intimately connected to both past and future'.[5] I can take this a step further and restate that only the past exists. Documents, like works of art, are physical examples of the past.

Within the context of the sub-title of this book, namely *Understanding Inter-state Relations*, primary source documents, as Guicciardini well knew, are the raw material of many a historian seeking to scrutinise and understand how and why events occur. When one begins to think about their implications, one starts to think by default about relations between states, and how diplomacy (and of course diplomats are not the only power brokers by any means) functions as the nuts and bolts of interstate relations. One sees how, albeit subconsciously, some international relations theory is sometimes practised by default, simply because of the plethora of think tanks that support (usually subtly) various government positions through their publications, positions which are then espoused by politicians and acted on by diplomats. Some politicians even write articles for journals such as *International Affairs* or *Foreign Affairs*, thus rubbing shoulders with respected academics, and gaining apparently intellectual kudos, as well as acceptance of, if not outright support for, sometimes unpopular policies. Although many of the diplomatic documents are written by professional diplomats, they reflect, especially in the case of Cyprus, a marked tendency towards political realism, particularly since their main concern is 'national interest', in other words acting in the perceived interests of the country they represent. They therefore tend to consider international relations in a state-centric manner, particularly since they themselves represent the state. This is so, even if they have not themselves studied international relations theory. They tend to be political realists if they are flexing their state's muscles, or practitioners of Bismarckian *Realpolitik*, if they are being more moderate. Before reaching the steppenwolfish relationship between the nation and the state, let us turn to the excavation and scrutiny of documents, the lifeblood of a geohistorian.

Documents

First, obtaining government documents can be like squeezing blood from a stone. This author spent over three years obtaining from the FCO certain documents on Cyprus, which should by law have been obtained much sooner. One of the most common excuses was: '[...] we believe the release of information in these folios would be likely to harm our relations with both Cyprus and the United States and that the public interest in maintaining good relations with these countries outweighs the public interest in disclosing it'.[6] I then contacted the Information Commissioner with my essential argument, namely: '[...] withholding such records is against the public interest, since this only increases the degree of ignorance and suspicion in certain quarters, which can in turn lead to misunderstandings and hostility, and to a lack of balance in historical analysis and evaluation, and even to the distortion of history. Moreover, it is difficult for a rational person to accept the FCOI arguments some thirty or forty years after the events that are being covered up/hidden/kept secret. The FCO arguments appear somewhat inconsistent in view of the mass of information that has emerged *recently* over the attack on Iraq, some of it officially inspired, not to mention officially inspired leaks on a whole range of issues with which the public is regularly fed through the media'.[7]

It was not until February 2008, well over three years after I had asked to see various documents and withheld folios, that the FCO was obliged to copy the documents and send them to me in Athens by courier. Better late than never. It would, however, have been better if when at the National Archives,[8] I had had access to the original documents, since there is no substitute to handling the originals, the very same files used thirty and more years ago by the officials handling the files. One can see the sequence of arguments, and how the nuts and bolts of policy formulation work, as well as handwritten comments in the margin, which can reveal the thinking of the officials, whether it be a minute, brief, policy paper or letter. We can see argument and counter-argument, for which no amount of reading of secondary sources can reproduce as effectively as seeing how events occurred and affected people. One feels that only history exists. There is no serious substitute for primary sources.

As one reads, then becomes now, which is itself becoming the past as we read. Most fascinating of all, as we read, we speculate as to what will happen in the next file or folio. Sometimes we predict with accuracy, but not always. We realise that the past includes speculation, assumptions and wishful thinking.

Given geohistory's contention that human characteristics and behaviour are the essential factors in policy formulation, with the state and its 'national' interests emanating from that, we begin to scrutinise the motives of the individuals, through what they are writing and, particularly important, through how they are writing, as well as why. The geohistorian detective will ask the following questions: why is the official writing? Is he responding/reacting, or initiating? Is he trying to please his superior? Has he omitted anything, or exaggerated? Is it worth researching him? Who actually wrote the letter? Was it the same person who signed it? Was the document written by an emotional foreign minister, or by a more rational desk officer? And who wrote on the sidelines of a typed document 'The Dutch Royal Family are persistent do-gooders', because the Netherlands was hosting a conference of the World Peace Council, which the FO considered to be a Soviet front organisation?

In sum, primary sources can, if treated with delicacy and circumspection, offer some insight into the minds of the writers of the documents, notwithstanding the constraints imposed by the demands of official writing. For example, in 1955, the British ambassador in Washington described the Greek ambassador as a snake.[9] Henry Kissinger was also described in unflattering terms by a senior official of the FCO: 'If to be a romantic is to admire great men [Metternich] who by cynical and ruthless action changed the course of history, then he is a romantic. He is also a romantic in the sense of seeing himself hopefully cutting as brilliant and successful a figure as those whom he admires. But it is quite clear for example from what we hear of his remarks in private that he enjoys making a cynical analysis of other people's capacities and motives, and is introspective and aware of the fact that he may have an incipient *folie de grandeur*'.[10] The reader of the file may well conclude that Kissinger was considered to be a bit of a cynic, with megalomaniacal tendencies.[11]

Here, we see the dichotomy of how, in the formulation of foreign policy, the politician is generally more emotional than the official, and how policy begins with the individual, which then becomes corporate, with the emotional, nationalistic elements being institutionalised and sanitised.

Another vital aspect of primary document research is revealing previously unknown facts, which expose previous government lies. One of the most celebrated is the Katyn massacre of Poles in 1940, which was considered until 1991 to have been perpetrated by the Nazis. When some of the Soviet archives were opened, the Russian government admitted that the crime had been perpetrated by the Soviet People's Commissariat for Internal Affairs.

Another revelation concerns FCO officials lying about foreknowledge of the Turkish invasion of Cyprus and actually advising a politician, Foreign Secretary James Callaghan, to be highly economical with the truth about his foreknowledge of both Turkish stages of the invasion. Callaghan and Kissinger were well aware on 10 August 1974 of Turkish plans to take over more than one-third of Cyprus.[12] But it is worth noting that Callaghan was also made aware on 19 July 1974 of the plan to undertake the first invasion of the following day: on the 19th, the Joint Intelligence Committee had informed Callaghan's Private Secretary of their expectation of an invasion 'in the next few days'.[13] Yet on 19 February 1976, when he appeared before the Parliamentary Select Committee on Cyprus and was asked whether he recognised that 'there was to be an immediate invasion by the Turks into at least northern Cyprus at the time and that that was imminent', he answered 'No'. And when asked whether 'events still continued to indicate that there was a real danger of further advance', he replied: 'No, I do not think that was indicated at all'.[14] This was despite his having been advised that the Turkish army was about to break out and take over one-third of the island.

Notwithstanding that this is essentially a polite academic book, it has to be said that if the documents in the British National Archives are genuine (and I cannot possibly see how they are not), then it does seem clear that the British Secretary of State for Foreign and Commonwealth Affairs denied the facts to a parliamentary committee. To compound his denial, he was accompanied by three FCO minders, namely the Head of Southern European Department, Alan Goodison, the Second Legal Adviser, John Freeland, and the head of Claims Department, Derrick Burden. One can immediately understand the presence of the first two officials, but not that of Burden. But when one thinks further, one sees that if Callaghan had admitted that he was aware of Turkish plans, he could then have been accused of not having protected the interests of thousands of Commonwealth citizens, not to mention a fair number of British subjects (most with Greek names) who lost their homes and who could therefore sue the British government for compensation. But there was of course even more to it than that. First, Callaghan was being groomed to take over the premiership from Harold Wilson, which he duly did two months later. Had the truth come out, his image of the solid, trustworthy avuncular politician would have been besmirched. More to the point, he could easily have been portrayed (with considerable justification, as we have seen) as having succumbed to Kissinger's 'suggestions', as well as to Turkey's bulldozing, particularly regarding the Treaty of Guarantee. And crucially, it would have embarrassed Kissinger, to whom Callaghan seemed beholden. To add to this tawdry tale of backstage double-dealing, it was during a particularly lively bout of Greek and Cypriot media speculation about the British rôle in the invasion that Callaghan (or, rather, his minders) instructed their embassy in Athens and High Commission in Nicosia to 'as necessary deny that HMG had any advance intelligence about the coup or the invasion', and to say that Callaghan had denied this to the Select Committee. It is little wonder that the report of the Parliamentary Select Committee on Cyprus stated unequivocally: 'Britain had a right to intervene, she had the moral obligation to intervene, she had the military capacity to intervene. She did not intervene for reasons which the Government refuses to give'.[15] The committee had probably not had access to the documents that I was able to obtain years later, however. Had they been able to, one can rightly wonder whether Callaghan would have become Prime Minister. Machiavelli would perhaps agree with the extreme form of *raison d'état* that this story shows.

Another example of facts emerging a long time after they occur is that between the Turkish invasion and 1980, Britain actually tried to give up its bases on Cyprus, but that Kissinger throttled the idea, giving the Arab-Israel dispute as a reason. Had any historian attempted to even suggest this before 2008, when I obtained various documents, he would surely would have been dismissed as a 'conspiracy theorist'.[16]

So much for the geohistorian's and Guicciardini's lifeblood, official documents. We should not of course forget other forms of literature. We now have to consider the steppenwolfish relationship between the state and the nation, and why atavism, nostalgia and identity play key rôles.

Atavism and Nostalgia

Atavism and nostalgia are key components to understanding relations between states through geohistory, connected to memory as they are, be that memory individual or corporate. This connects to geohistory's contention that the starting point and basis of understanding relations between states are the individual, in other words the 'twigs in the wood of the state'. But before we consider atavism and nostalgia, connected as they are to emotion, let us define 'nation' and 'state' as unpolemically and simply as we can.

Etymologically speaking, a nation is where one is born. Nowadays, a nation is a group of people of similar language, culture, religion, blood and heritage, usually born in the same area. As such, very few nations correspond precisely to state borders. Perhaps the Jewish State can claim to be, since the majority of its inhabitants are Jewish. The question becomes tricky, however, when one considers that more Jews reside outside the Jewish State than inside it. In this sense, the Jewish nation covers most countries of the world. Mass movements of populations have rendered a completely precise definition of a nation difficult. For example, when an American president speaks of the American nation, one can wonder whether he means anyone born in the US, which includes original indigenous tribes and elements of various other nations, or whether he really means 'state', but prefers the more emotional sounding 'nation'.

The concept of state is simpler: a group of peoples living within a defined and internationally recognised border, with its own government and sovereignty. As such, territory is the essential factor. We know enough about the ancient Greek city states and Renaissance Italy to see that states based on territory have existed for a long time. One can also argue that pre-imperial England and France were states, rather than empires. But when we come to the term 'nation-state', matters become complicated.

First, many IR analysts, often of the realist school, use the words 'nation' and 'state' interchangeably. A way of avoiding this ambiguity is to use the word 'country', but even that is vague. To confuse the issue, politicians and others use the term 'national interest', when they really mean 'state interest' (we shall discuss 'interests' a little later). Even the term 'international relations' lacks in precision, since it really means 'inter-state relations'.

Unlike with the word 'state', it is difficult to come to terms with the term (pardon the pun) 'nation-state'; it seems to be an utopian ideal at best or an oxymoron at worst. The fixation with the Peace of Westphalia of 1648 by many IR analysts and historians has rather muddied the waters, since there are claims that the concept of sovereignty arose out of the various associated treaties. While it is true that various sovereign German states were created out of the Holy Roman Empire, and that they were able to choose whether to be Roman Catholic or Protestant, and that the principle of equality between states was established, Jean Bodin had already established the concept of sovereignty in 1576, in his work *Les Six Livres de la République*, in which he argued that a state should be sovereign. There are also differing interpretations of sovereignty, perhaps one of the more extreme versions being encapsulated in Louis XIV's statement 'L'état, c'est moi'. A geohistorian might prefer the word 'independence'. But for all the Peace of Westphalia's contribution to the idea of sovereign states respecting each other's sovereignty, it could even be argued that it served as a failed attempt to establish a permanent peace, since in fact it led to further strife, this time between nominally sovereign countries, perhaps because de Groot's ideas on international law, encapsulated in his book 'On the Law of War and Peace', published in 1625, were not to every sovereign state's liking.

As to the idea of Westphalian religious freedom, in 1685, France revoked the Edict of Nantes, which guaranteed freedom of worship to Protestants in 1598, and England continued to discriminate against Roman Catholics until well into the nineteenth century. Religion and nationalism continue to be a problem to this day, as the case of the break-up of Yugoslavia and, at a world level, Moslem fundamentalism and Christian Zionism demonstrate. Attempts to create states based on nations have failed, as, for example, the case of the Kurds and Yugoslavia dramatically show, and continue to show, and as a glimpse at Albanian nationalism, Bosnia-Herzegovina and Macedonia show. The nation-state is simply an ideal, rendered impossible because the word 'nation', with its emotional content, clashes with the cold and rational state. A homogenous nation governed by its own sovereign state is more of an ideal than a reality, although Iceland and Japan may claim to a measure of convergence between state and nation.

Individual and corporate human characteristics count for little in the dreams and ambitions of armchair geostrategists pursuing state interests. In their planning, they avoid atavism and nostalgia, key components of geohistory. The gap between their pursuit of state interests and the reality of human characteristics remains.

Although nostalgia and atavism affect both individuals and states, neither appear in *The Penguin Dictionary of International Relations*. They nevertheless form a central component of geohistory's emphasis on individual and corporate characteristics in understanding inter-state behaviour, interests included. One aspect of nostalgia is a longing for past events, which connects it to atavism and nationalism. It affects nations, often detrimentally, particularly when a state structure is not strong and deep enough to prevent outbursts both in its own state and in nostalgic and atavistic claims on neighbouring ones. A good example is the Greek 'Megali Idea' (expanding the Greek state to include the Eastern Roman Empire by taking it back from the Ottomans), whereby a combination of nationalism, fuelled by nostalgia and its political exploiters, Venizelos and Lloyd George, led to the 'Great Catastrophe' and the killing and expulsion from Asia Minor of around one and a half million Ottoman citizens of Greek stock and religion, as well as Armenians and Syriacs. In the end, the cold *raison d'état* of the British Foreign Office, the Quai d'Orsay and the clever Italians put paid to the wild dream. Another example of the power of nostalgia and atavism is the break-up of Yugoslavia in the 1990s, when pent up religious and ethnic forces exploded (with outside interference). Notwithstanding this outside interference, playing on people's atavism was key, and even some of the outside meddlers were not immune to their own atavism, given the rôle of the Vatican and atavistic German business interests.[17] Other examples of atavism, connected to nostalgia, are 'neo-Ottomanism' and Italy's harking back to the Roman Empire, mainly during Mussolini's day. Readers of this book can doubtless think of plenty of other examples.

IDENTITY

I shall not insult the reader's intelligence and define the word identity itself. At state level, identity has generally developed by default. For example, the so-called One Hundred Years War[18] began as a dynastic and territorial dispute between royal relatives, but ended up by defining England and France. It was during this war that English was made England's official language, and Englishmen and Frenchmen could identify themselves as such. As for Italian identity, it is as old as the Roman Empire as a geographical name, a name enhanced emotionally by Machiavelli.

We can also state here (no pun intended) that the younger the state, the more a feeling of insecurity. One example is Turkey, less than one hundred years old at the time of writing. Again, the archives come to our aid here (see Chapter 6): 'Leaving aside Istanbul and Izmir and the Aegean littoral, for my money Turkey is more of the Near East and Asia than Europe. Not just physically, with 97% of its territory in Asia, but temperamentally. Politically of course, so far as the central direction if affairs is concerned, it looks to Europe and sees itself as Europe and wants others to see it so—which indeed they have done: what British schoolboy has not heard of the Sick Man of Europe? [...] Perhaps this deliberate cultivation of a Western outlook, with all that it means in education, has led the ruling circles and intellectuals and industrialists to regard themselves as truly European, and Turkey in general as Western. [...] There is no natural reason why the Turks should be so insistent on their European connexion. It is largely the dictum of Kamal Atatürk that makes them'. [...] 'Although to speak of an identity crisis would be rather strong, it is certainly arguable that the younger the state, the more the quest to seek an identity'.[19]

Now, Turkey has reverted to 'neo-Ottomanism' and a strong element of nationalism, which can sometimes go hand in hand with the quest for identity. This is accompanied by what can be called a 'Sèvres complex', which still lurks in the back of the minds of nationalist Turks: by the Treaty of Sèvres of 1920, Turkey would have been far smaller than today, and the Kurds would have been allowed to hold a referendum on independence. It can nevertheless be agreed that modern Turkey came about through circumstances which were not artificially created, and where the survival of the language despite the change to the Roman alphabet was assured. As regards artificial states, we can turn to the case of North Macedonia (see Chapter 6). Readers of this book can surely locate other examples of the links between atavism and identity. We can also observe that identity often impinges on state and nation at the same time, and that the greater the degree of insecurity, whether at individual or state level, the more the quest to define an identity. It is certainly true that the younger the state, the more the quest to seek an identity.

Identity has, however, recently become one of the most exploited terms in politics, in the shape of 'identity politics', studied mainly at various Anglo-Saxon universities. This has muddied the waters for those seeking clarity. It is a recent phenomenon of globalisation and digitalisation, and the concomitant tendency to categorise groups. It is here that, in line with geohistory, we drop to the level of the individual being categorised as a member of a particular group, often created by external political forces in the name of freedom. Sometimes, one group's claims to feeling threatened and voiceless attract another group's derision because it dismisses their own feelings of persecution—but such is the nature of political tribalism.

Gender politics is part of this categorisation process and has led to all manner of disputes. At my last count, some universities were teaching that there are twenty-six genders. The number is probably increasing as you read this. A humourist might conclude that there are as many genders as people. This all boils down to a feeling being inculcated into people that they must have a group identity. A geohistorian would posit that this is an example of social engineering and an attempt to alter the natural identity which an individual develops from birth, to 'empower' him and to mould him into a category that can be easily managed. 'Divide and rule' comes to mind. This is not to suggest that there is a coven of multi-billionaires plotting to take over the world, but rather an observation as to recent developments. The reader needs to take this geohistorical argumentation as a thought stimulant, perhaps wondering what happened to the adage 'live and let live', and the idea of male and female.

As we hopefully begin to see the importance of understanding individual human characteristics and behaviour in inter-state relations, we can better understand nationalism.

Nationalism

Academics and others have been dissecting the term 'nationalism' for many years, leading to an element of confusion. We shall try to keep matters simple. One kind is fairly obvious, encapsulated in Shakespeare's: 'Cry God for Harry! England! and Saint George!'[20] In other words, it can be a cause of war and even vice versa. This is an immutable part of geohistory and is predicated on strengthening one's identity through hostility towards another nation or state. At a lower level, the dark side of tribalism is an ingredient of nationalism. One example of nationalism is that of Americans stoning Dachshunds to death after the sinking of the Lusitania in 1917. A good recent case is Brexit, where pro-Brexiteers appealed to voters' emotions, using a perhaps exaggerated concept of sovereignty and immigration, but tending to downplay the economic disadvantages of leaving the EU. Such examples cover the emotional side, often exploited by government propaganda to instil a feeling of hostility in individuals, towards a foreign country. In reality, we are talking about state interests here, in the sense that a nation can be an emotional version of the state.

It is, however, difficult to escape from the semantic straightjacket of the unquestioning usage of the word 'nation' to mean 'state', and vice versa, over many years.

Nationalism also has an ideological sense, in that it can be connected to the fight for self-determination and independence. The French Revolution led to this modern version of nationalism. Napoleon, for example, established the Kingdom of Italy.[21] This served as an impetus for the Risorgimento and then the fight for Greek independence, as well as revolutionary movements throughout the nineteenth century. In the period 1815 to 1919, national movements led to the break-up of the Austro-Hungarian and Ottoman empires. Nationalism as a force remained, particularly under the rubric of 'self-determination', as enunciated in the Treaty of Versailles.[22] Self-determination can serve as a euphemism for nationalism.

The emotional side of nationalism is related to people's characteristics per se, individual and then corporate, which are played on either by governments or independently, by free choice. Similarly, the ideological version of nationalism is also related to individual and corporate characteristics, in that self-determination and freedom are determined by characteristics such as nostalgia, and the behaviour that results.

Having ploughed through nostalgia, atavism, identity, the nation, the state and nationalism, we begin to arrive at the crux of this book: interests.

NATIONAL OR STATE INTERESTS?

British Secretary of State Palmerston is well known for his statement that 'we have no eternal allies and no perpetual enemies. Our interests are eternal and perpetual, and those interests it is our duty to follow'.[23] It is unlikely that he was talking about the interests of parts of the British Empire, India etc., but more likely referring to England. He can be described as a nationalist of the jingoistic kind, revered today by realists of the ilk of Henry Kissinger.[24] For the purposes of geohistory, however, by national interests we really mean state interests, unlike in the case of nationalists seeking to create their own state. Defining state interests is not easy. From this author's experience (he spent six years as a British diplomat), it can include bowing to American pressure to leave UNESCO ('slipstream diplomacy'); agreeing to convince the Dutch government to install US missiles on their territory; reporting on any perceived anti-British activity; looking out for any anti-British feeling and visiting officials to put the British viewpoint; delivering grey propaganda in a brown envelope to 'trusted contacts' in the Dutch media and elsewhere[25]; and negotiating British views at United Nations conferences. The importance of dispassion in carrying out a task is constantly emphasised.

Territorial integrity and the acquisition of the resources necessary to ensure the power of the state are the basis of the 'national' (i.e. state) interest, which therefore connects to *raison d'etat*. Although morality is often used as a tool, this needs to be taken with a pinch of salt; plenty of wars fought over control of resources have claimed to be humanitarian. Let us turn to literature to make the point: 'A certain sentimentality is the common coin of political debate. Nations [states?] are governed by self-interest, but they prefer to believe that their aims are altruistic, and the politician is justified if with fair words and fine phrases he can persuade the electorate that the hard bargain he is driving for his county's advantage tends to the good of humanity'.[26] In this connexion, Guicciardini writes: 'Distrust all those who talk loudly of liberty: for nearly all of them, aye all of them without exception, have their own ends to serve'.[27]

At the risk of frightening readers, I submit that the following can be considered as the pursuit of state interests gone over the emotional and sometimes tribal nationalist top: the destruction of Milos (Athens); the murder of Irish priests, woman and children at Wexford and Drogheda (England); the Amritsar massacre (Britain); the genocide of Armenians, Greeks and Syriacs (Ottoman Empire); the genocide of the Amerindians and the My Lai massacre (US); the shooting of Polish prisoners (Soviet Union); the genocide of gypsies and Hebrews (Germany); the bombing of Dresden (the US by day, Britain by night), and of Hiroshima and Nagasaki (US); the genocide of Serbs (Croatia), of Cambodians (Cambodia) and of Tutsis (Ruanda); and the butchering of Palestinians at Shatah, Sabrila and elsewhere (Israel). There are many others.

Given that the acquisition of resources is a central component of state ('national') interests and of geopolitics, it follows that war often results from the greed engendered by a geopolitical mindset. We touch now on the crux of this book: a geopolitician's counterargument to a geohistorian's would run something like this: 'What a geohistorian sees as human history repeating itself, even if in different colours and names, is in fact the work of national interests at play. States get into repeated quarrels because their interests—geopolitical, economic, religious or ideological—are repeatedly challenged. The human natures of the actors involved do not matter much'.

A geohistorian will reply that the concept of national interest has been unquestioned for too long, and has coagulated, affecting the minds of policy formulators, and that the answer lies in the immutable characteristics of human beings and the unpredictable behaviour emanating therefrom. Put more bluntly, the current jaded concept of national interest is used as an excuse for war and needs to be considered within the context of greed, insecurity, pride, anger, jealousy and ambition, which can be seen as the most basic causes of war, with national interest disguising state interest as the reason and justification. Pride and face-saving play an oft underestimated rôle in the outbreak of wars, which then gather their own automatic momentum. These characteristics affect the cold and allegedly reasonable policy formulators and leaders, as they do the general population. As for the idea of states' interests being challenged, this is too simplistic an assumption, since feelings of suspicion, emotion and insecurity are often the triggers, rather than national interests per se. Little wonder that Machiavelli is used by out and out geopoliticians and power politicians. Guicciardini is more moderate and less damning of the human race. His idea of maintaining some sort of stability between power centres is more thoughtful than the automatic assumption that only state interests matter. Thus, today, a geopolitician will advocate a political solution, while a geohistorian will opt for a legal one, since the latter is more likely to avoid war, unlike the implied illegality and danger contained in a political solution.[28] Here, we must turn, albeit briefly, to foreign policy, diplomacy and secrecy.

FOREIGN POLICY, DIPLOMACY AND SECRECY

Although diplomacy has come under increasing attack in recent years, it is still the nuts and bolts of inter-state relations, despite the encroachment of big business interests and the power of worldwide organisations. Let us go back to the ever-disappearing basics: 'If truthfulness be the first essential of the ideal diplomatist, the second essential is precision. By this is meant not merely intellectual accuracy, but moral accuracy. The negotiator should be accurate both in mind and soul'.[29] Nicolson goes on to argue that while the details of negotiation should be kept necessarily out of the public eye, policy aims should not. This connects to Canning and his 'antithesis', Palmerston: 'To a diplomatist of the old school such as Metternich the very idea that the public should have any knowledge of, or opinion upon, foreign policy, appeared both dangerous and fantastic. Canning, on the other hand, regarded public opinion as something which, so far from being avoided, should actually be invoked. It was mainly for this reason that Metternich described him as "a malevolent factor hurled by divine providence upon Europe"'.[30]

Common sense suggests that the more the need for complete secrecy in government, the greater the feeling of insecurity in the state. It seems that we have not moved much further since Guicciardini's day, and that secrecy is still an integral part of inter-state relations.[31] Globalisation, digitalisation and a geopolitical mentality have, however, altered matters dramatically, with the advent of WikiLeaks and other forms of exposure. The answer is to keep the details of inter-state negotiations private, but to make the objectives public. And when and if state skulduggery is exposed, either years later through historians, or through more immediate unconventional electronic means, then the state concerned should explain and apologise. As regards state spying agencies such as the CIA and Britain's MI6, the less the parliamentary control and accountability, the more dangerous they can be to balanced relations between states. The Iraq horror, which has continued to bedevil inter-state relations, says it all. Had MI6 had some integrity, or at least been accountable, it would have seen off Blair's cheating, and the US would have thought twice about the illegal war. And had the study of foreign policy per se been accorded a higher position, rather than the vague term 'international relations', perhaps Guicciardinian reflexion and caution would have won the day. Regarding diplomacy, the speed of globalisation is now counteracting what diplomats should be. Successful negotiation should be based not on Twitter, but on seven specific diplomatic virtues: truthfulness, precision, calm, good temper, patience, modesty and loyalty.[32] Instead, we have been offered the nationalistic emotion of Bush Jr, with his talk of a crusade and exporting freedom, with harassed diplomats having their hands tied. The fanatics took over.

Any studies on foreign policy and diplomacy should include literature, simply to gain understanding of those with whom one is negotiating: 'His practice was to draw the attention of his students to three French writers who in his opinion combined the qualities that are the mainsprings of the French character. By reading them, he said, you could learn so much about the French people that, if he had the power, he would not trust such of our rulers as have to deal with the French nation to enter upon their offices till they had passed a pretty stiff examination on their works'.[33] Similarly, Leo Tolstoy gives us insights into both Russian and, vicariously, German, thinking: 'A Russian is self-assured just because he knows nothing and does not want to know anything, since he does not believe that anything can be known. The German's self-assurance is worst of all, stronger and more repulsive than any other, because he imagines that he knows the truth – science – which has himself invented but which is for him the absolute truth'.[34] I do not have the space to elaborate on this, but leave it to the reader to do so. We must conclude.

Conclusions

'History is the life of nations and humanity. To seize and put into words, to describe directly, the life of humanity or even of a single nation appears impossible. [...] For history, lines exist of the movement of human wills, one end of which is hidden in the unknown but at the other end of which a consciousness of man's will in the present moves in space, time, and dependence on cause'.[35] We see here the juxtaposition of the unknown with reason, and a connexion to Guicciardini who, whatever his understanding of *raison d'état*, wrote that men are not ruled by reason.

It is thus to human characteristics that we must turn if we are to better understand why over-reliance on state interests is exaggerated in the analysis of inter-state relations. The unquestioning acceptance of state interests as a starting point for understanding is misplaced, since it is characteristics such as greed, pride, vanity, jealousy, anger, insecurity, prejudice, ambition and idealism which determine the state of humanity and state interests. The globalisation of geopolitics in the name of unification has oxymoronically led to the weakening of the state and the strengthening of fragmentation and extreme nationalism, in the seductive name of 'a world without borders', when it is well enough known that good fences make good neighbours. Yet this geohistorical common sense evades the geopoliticians, with the speed of technology destroying the art of Guicciardinian caution and balance, and where greed is increasing and leading to a renewed emphasis on interests, as if they are the be-all and end-all of human existence. As for the steppenwolfish relationship between state and nation, and the idealistic assumption that the (confusing) concept of the nation-state is viable, ne'er the twain shall meet. People, with their immutable characteristics and unpredictable behaviour, create events, on which interests are only then predicated.

Better, therefore, to base all on the unemotional and dispassionate state as the only arbiter between the diverse groups that inhabit it, with equal rights for everybody, without the need to alienate group from group through the exploitation of identity politics, over-categorisation and nationalism. The state, currently under threat, is the only guarantee against chaos that we have in an increasingly confused world of emotional, political and ideological 'isms'.

Heaven forbid that geohistory, which helps to balance reason with the unpredictable, become yet another theory, to be dissected, placed in a

8 THE RICORDI AND MEMORY   137

paradigm, and tried and tested. It is simply an approach to slow down the current thoughtless spiral of globalised geopolitics and to understand the misnomer 'national' interests. As with Guicciardini, let experience be our guide.

I realise that this book may have touched some nerves, raw or otherwise. And if it has, then I shall have at least succeeded in provoking some serious, ideology-free thinking, whatever howls of protest there may be. I leave the last word with Francesco Guicciardini: 'In my youth I believed that no amount of reflection would enable me to see more than I took in at a glance. But experience has shown me this opinion to be utterly false; and you may laugh at anyone who maintains the contrary. The longer we reflect, the clearer things grow and the better we understand them'.[36] 'The affairs of this world are so shifting, and depend on so many accidents, that it is hard to form any judgment concerning the future' (Fig. 8.1).[37]

Fig. 8.1 Guicciardini through the Ages, by the artist-illustrator Alice Mallinson

Notes

1. Mallinson, William, *Public Lies and Private Truths*, Cassel, 1996.
2. Vico, Giambattista, *New Science: Principles of the New Science Concerning the Common Nature of Nations*, Penguin Books, London and New York etc., 1999, p. 154.
3. Taylor, A.J.P., *The Origins of the Second World War*, Penguin Books Ltd., London, 1964, pp. 8–9.
4. Hill, Christopher, *The Changing Politics of Foreign Policy*, Palgrave Macmillan, Basingstoke, 2003, pp. 116–117.
5. Ibid., p. 117.
6. Prior, Penny (Information Management Group, FCO) to author, 10 March 2005, *letter*.
7. Author to Information Commissioner, 23 February 2006, *letter*.
8. I prefer the former term 'Public Record Office'.
9. Ward, 27 April 1955, BNA FO 371/117625, file RG 1001/243/9, *memorandum*.
10. Cable to Acland, 31 July 1973, BNA PREM 15/1983, *minute*.
11. I am unable to resist quoting Oscar Wilde's definition of a cynic: 'A cynic is a man who knows the price of everything, and the value of nothing'. As it happens, Kissinger studied accountancy.
12. Mellersh [Vice-Chief of Defence Staff for Operations] to Secretary of State, 10 August 1974, *memorandum*, BNA-FCO 9/1915, file WSC 1/10, part Z.
13. Thomson to Private Secretary, *record of meeting*, BNA-FCO 9/1984, file WSC 1/10, part E.
14. *The Select Committee on Cyprus: Minutes of Evidence*, Thursday, 19th February, 1976, BNA-FCO 9/2192, file WSC 3/548/10, part C.
15. Mirbagheri, Farid, *Cyprus and International Peacekeeping*, C. Hurst & Co., London, 1998, pp. 102–103.
16. Mallinson, William, *Kissinger and the Invasion of Cyprus*, Cambridge Scholars Publishing, Newcastle upon Tyne, 2016, 2017, Chapter 7.
17. Here, one can argue that Germany took over from the Austro-Hungarian empire in its hostility towards Serbia. As for the Vatican's premature recognition of Roman Catholic Croatia, it led to the 'me-too' effect and murderous wars.
18. It actually lasted 137 years, followed by a series of wars that did not stop until 1814, with the Battle of Waterloo.
19. Phillips to Secretary of State, 31 May 1977; *Diplomatic Report* no. 215/77, NA-FCO 9/2669, file WST 014/1, part B, in Mallinson, William, *Thrice a Stranger: Penelope's Easter Mediterranean Odyssey*, Cambridge Scholars Publishing, Newcastle upon Tyne, 2016, p. 71.
20. *Henry V*, Act III, Scene I.

21. He also made his brother-in-law King of Naples.
22. Rush, Michael, *Politics and Society*, Prentice Hall Harvester Wheatsheaf, Hemel Hempstead, 1992, p. 35.
23. Dickie, John, *Inside the Foreign Office*, Chapmans, London, 1992, p. 42.
24. Kissinger, Henry, *Diplomacy*, Simon and Schuster Paperbacks, New York, 1994, pp. 162–163. He gives a brief but interesting analysis of the differences in Palmerstone's and Gladstone's approach, claiming that the former saw the Concert of Europe as a tool for preserving the balance of power, while the latter saw it as a way to bring about a new world order. Perhaps he was slightly exaggerating Gladstone's ideas. Gladstone's invasion of Egypt hardly equates with establishing a new world order!
25. Information Research Department (IRD) was set up in the FCO in 1947 to spread anti-Soviet messages. Moscow's reaction was to set up the COMINFORM. IRD was wound up in 1977 by the then Secretary of State, David Owen, but probably still exists in other forms.
26. Somerset Maugham, William, 'Lord Mountdrago', *Collected Short Stories*, Volume Two, Pan Books Ltd., London, 1982 (First published by William Heinemann Ltd.), 1951, pp. 283–284.
27. Guicciardini, Francesco, *Counsels and Reflections*, translated from the Italian (*Ricordi Politici e Civili*) by Ninian Hill Thomson, M.A., Kegan Paul, Trench Trübner & Co., Ltd., London, 1890, 66, p. 33.
28. Turkey has been hankering for a political solution to its claims on Greek territory. 'They [the Turks] can presumably not have very much confidence in winning their case at the Court on its merits alone.' Fullerton to Wright, *letter*, 28 September 1975, BNA FCO 9/2233, file WSG 3/318/1.
29. Nicolson, Harold, *Diplomacy*, Oxford University Press, 1969, p. 60. Guicciardini writes: 'For the minister of a prince, I mean one who has to serve him in affairs of moment, must not only be of great capacity, and such men are rare, but must also be of sterling honesty, a qualification perhaps even rarer than the other', 3, pp. 4–5.
30. Ibid., p. 37.
31. ''Tis incredible how much it profits a ruler that he observe secrecy in the conduct of his affairs. For besides that were his designs known they might be forestalled or thwarted, the very fact that men are in ignorance of them keeps them in suspense and wonder [...] in addition to all the other injuries it may do you to have your secrets known, you become the slave of those to whom you confide them.' Op. cit., Guicciardini, *Ricordi*, 270, 271, pp. 114–115.
32. Op. cit., Nicolson, p. 55.
33. Somerset Maugham, William, 'Appearance and Reality' *Collected Short Stories*, Volume 1, Penguin Books, 1977, p. 175, first published by William Heinemann Ltd., London, 1951.

34. Tolstoy, Leo, *War and Peace*, (translated by Louise and Aylmer Maude), Wordsworth Editions Limited, Ware, Hertfordshire, 2001; Second Epilogue p. 505. First published its entirety in Moscow in 1869.
35. Ibid., p. 929.
36. Op. cit., Guicciardini, *Ricordi*, 297, p. 126.
37. Ibid., 318, p. 134.

Bibliography

Dickie, John, Inside the Foreign Office, Chapmans, London, 1992.
Guicciardini, Francesco, *Counsels and Reflections*, translated from the Italian (*Ricordi Politici e Civili*) by Ninian Hill Thomson, M.A., Kegan Paul, Trench Trübner & Co., Ltd., London, 1890.
Hill, Christopher, The Changing Politics of Foreign Policy, Palgrave Macmillan, Basingstoke, 2003.
Kissinger, Henry, Diplomacy, Simon and Schuster Paperbacks, New York, 1994.
Mallinson, William, Kissinger and the Invasion of Cyprus, Cambridge Scholars Publishing, Newcastle upon Tyne, 2016, 2017.
Mallinson, William, Public Lies and Private Truths, Cassel, 1996.
Mirbagheri, Farid, Cyprus and International Peacekeeping, C. Hurst & Co., London 1998.
Nicolson, Harold, Diplomacy, Oxford University Press, 1969.
Rush, Michael, Politics and Society, Prentice Hall Harvester Wheatsheaf, Hemel Hempstead, 1992.
Somerset Maugham, William, 'Lord Mountdrago', Collected Short Stories, Volume Two, Pan Books Ltd., London, 1982 (First published by William Heinemann Ltd.), 1951.
Somerset Maugham, William, 'Appearance and Reality' Collected Short Stories, Volume 1, Penguin Books, 1977, p. 175, first published by William Heinemann Ltd., London, 1951.
Taylor, A.J.P., The Origins of the Second World War, Penguin Books Ltd., London, 1964.
Tolstoy, Leo, War and Peace, (translated by Louise and Aylmer Maude), Wordsworth Editions Limited, Ware, Hertfordshire, 2001.
Vico, Giambattista, New Science: Principles of the New Science Concerning the Common Nature of Nations, Penguin Books, London, New York etc., 1999.

Bibliography

Books

Aristotle, *The Art of Rhetoric*, translated and introduced by Lawson Tancred, H. C., Penguin Books, London, 1991.

Barzini, Luigi, *The Italians*, Bantam Books, 1965, published by arrangement with the original publishers, Atheneum Publishers, 1964.

Berridge, G. R., *International Politics*, Pearson Education, Harlow, 2002.

Buckle, B. E., *The Life of Benjamin Disraeli, Earl of Beaconsfield*, John Murray, London, 1920.

Brzezinski, Zbigniew, *The Grand Chessboard: American Primacy and Its Geopolitical Imperatives*, Basic Books, New York, 1997.

Butterfield, Herbert and Wight, Martin (eds.) *Diplomatic Investigations*, George Allen & Unwin Ltd., London, 1966.

Christie, Agatha, *The ABC Murders*, Pan Books, London, 1958 (first published in 1936).

Clogg, Richard, *A Concise History of Greece*, Cambridge University Press, 1992.

Dugin, Alexandr, *Foundations of Geopolitics*, Arctogaia, Moscow, 1997.

Dickie, John, *Inside the Foreign Office*, Chapmans, London, 1992.

Evans, Graham and Newnham, Jeffrey, *The Penguin Dictionary of International Relations*, Penguin, London etc., 1998.

Fouskas, Vassilis K., *Zones of Conflict*, Pluto Press, London, Sterling, Virginia, 2003.

Giddens, Anthony, *The Third Way: The Renewal of Social Democracy*, Wiley, 1998.

Gat, Azar, *The Origins of Military Thought*, Oxford University Press, 1989.
Goffman, Erving, *The Presentation of Self in Everyday Life*, Penguin, 1984.
Grunig, James E. and Hunt, Todd, *Managing Public Relations*, Holt, Rinehart and Winston, New York, 1984.
Guicciardini, Francesco, *Counsels and Reflections*, translated from the Italian (*Ricordi Politici e Civili*) by Ninian Hill Thomson, M.A., Kegan Paul, Trench Trübner & Co., Ltd., London, 1890.
Guicciardini, Francesco, *History of Italy*, republished by BiblioLife, 2009.
Hill, Christopher, *The Changing Politics of Foreign Policy*, Palgrave Macmillan, Basingstoke, 2003.
Huttenback, Robert A., *Racism and Empire*, Cornell University Press, Ithaca and London, 1976.
Irving, David, *Churchill's War*, vol. 1, Arrow Books, London, 1989.
Kissinger, Henry, *Diplomacy*, Simon and Schuster Paperbacks, New York, 1994.
Kissinger, Henry A., *Nuclear Weapons and Foreign Policy*, Harper and Brothers, New York, 1957.
Kissinger, Henry, *World Order*, Allen Lane, London, 2014.
Lasch, Christopher, *The Revolt of the Elites*, W.W. Norton & Company, New York and London, 1995.
Lawrence, D.H., *Lady Chatterley's Lover*, Penguin Books Ltd., 1960.
Le Carré, John, *Absolute Friends*, Coronet Books (Hodder and Stoughton), London, 2004.
Machiavelli, Niccolò, *The Prince*, Oxford University Press, 1990.
Mahan, Alfred Thayer, *The Problem of Asia and the Effects upon International Politics*, Konikat Press, Washington and London, 1920.
Mallinson, Bill, *Public Lies and Private Truths: An Anatomy of Public Relations*, Cassell, London and New York, 1996, and Leader Books, Athens, 2000.
Mallinson, William, *Cyprus: A Modern History*, I.B. Tauris, London and New York, 2005, 2009, 2012.
Mallinson, William, *Cyprus: Diplomatic History and the Clash of Theory International Relations*, I.B. Tauris, London and New York, 2010.
Mallinson, William, *Behind the Words: The FCO, Hegemonolingualism and the End of Britain's Freedom*, Cambridge Scholars Publishing, Newcastle upon Tyne, 2014.
Mallinson, William, *Kissinger and the Invasion of Cyprus: Diplomacy in the Eastern Mediterranean*, Cambridge Scholars Publishing, Newcastle upon Tyne, 2016 and 2017.
Mallinson, William, *Images in Words: Only History Exists*, Cambridge Scholars Publishing, Newcastle upon Tyne, 2018.
Mallinson, William, *Thrice a Stranger*, Cambridge Scholars Publishing, Newcastle upon Tyne, 2016, 2017.

Mallinson, William, *Britain and Cyprus: Key Themes and Documents since World War Two*, I. B. Tauris, London and New York, 2011. Republished by Bloomsbury Academic, London, 2020.

Mallinson, William and Ristic, Zoran, *The Threat of Geopolitics to International Relations: Obsession with the Heartland*, Cambridge Scholars Publishing, Newcastle upon upon Tyne, 2016 and 2017.

Markides, Diana, *Cyprus 1957–1963; from Colonial Conflict to Constitutional Crisis: The Key Role of the Municipal Issue*, Minneapolis, MI, 2001.

Mirbagheri, Farid, *Cyprus and International Peacekeeping*, C. Hurst & Co., London 1998.

Nicolson, Harold, *Diplomacy*, Oxford University Press, 1969.

Noel-Baker, Francis, *Greece: The Whole Story*, Hutchinson & Co., London, 1946.

O'Malley, Brendan and Craig, Ian, *The Cyprus Conspiracy*, I. B. Tauris, London and New York, 1999.

Ó Tuathail, Gearóid, Dalby, Simon and Routledge, Paul, *The Geopolitics Reader*, Routledge, London and New York, 1998.

Parenti, Michael, *Inventing Reality*, St. Martin's Press, New York, 1993.

Platias, Athanassios G., and Koliopoulos, Constantinos, *Thucydides on Strategy*, Hurst and Company, London, 2010.

Rush, Michael, *Politics and Society*, Prentice Hall Harvester Wheatsheaf, Hemel Hempstead, 1992.

Somerset Maugham, William, *Cakes and Ale*, Vintage Books, London, 2000, p. 23. First published by William Heinemann in 1930.

Somerset Maugham, William, *Collected Short Stories*, Volume One, Penguin Books, 1977, p. 175, first published by William Heinemann Ltd., London, 1951.

Somerset Maugham, William, *Collected Short Stories*, Volume Two, Pan Books Ltd., London, 1982 (First published by William Heinemann Ltd.), 1951.

Somerset Maugham, William, *Collected Short Stories*, vol. 1, Penguin Books, Harmondsworth, 1970 (1st edn.), William Heinemann, London, 1951.

Sked, Alan (ed.), *Europe's Balance of Power, 1815-1848*, Macmillan, London, 1979.

Spykman, Nicholas John, *The Geography of the Peace*, Harcourt, Brace and Company, New York, 1944.

Strathern, Paul, *The Medici*, Pimlico, London, 2005, p. 308; first published by Jonathan Cape, London, 2003.

Strauss, Leo and Cropsey, Joseph (eds.), *History of Political Philosophy*, University of Chicago, 1987 (first published in 1963).

Taylor, A.J.P., *Europe: Grandeur and Decline*, Penguin Books, London, New York etc., 1967 (first published in three volumes, 1950, 1952 and 1956).

Taylor, A.J.P., *The Origins of the Second World War*, Penguin Books Ltd., London, 1964.

Thucydides, *History of the Peloponnesian War*, translated by Rex Warner, introduction and notes by M. I. Finlay, Penguin Books, London, 1972.
Tolstoy, Leo, *War and Peace*, (translated by Louise and Aylmer Maude), Wordsworth Editions Limited, Ware, Hertfordshire, 2001; Second Epilogue p. 505. First published its entirety in Moscow in 1869.
Vico, Giambattista, *New Science: Principles of the New Science Concerning the Common Nature of Nations*, Penguin Books, London, New York etc., 1999, reprinted with corrections 2001, taken from the third edition of 1744; translated by David Marsh.
Wallbank, T. Walter et al. (eds.), *Civilisation, Past and Present*, vol. II, HarperCollins, 1996.
Wilde, Oscar, *The Works of Oscar Wilde*, Collins, London, 1948.
Woodhouse, C.M., *The Struggle for Greece, 1941–1949*, C. Hurst and Co. Ltd., London, 2002, originally published in 1976 by Hart-Davis, MacGibbon Ltd.
Yutang, Lin, *The Importance of Living*, William Heinemann Ltd., London, 1976. First published by John Day/Reynals and Hitchcock, New York, 1937.

Journals, Magazines and Newspapers

Bagehot, *The Economist*, 27 January 2011.
Bell, Duncan, 'Beware of False Prophets: Biology, Human Nature and the Future of International Relations Theory', *International Affairs*, Vol. 82, No. 3, Chatham House, London, May 2006.
Byman, Daniel, 'After the Storm: US Policy Toward Iraq Since 1991', *Political Science Quarterly*, vol. 115, No. 4, Winter 2000–2001.
Carruthers, Susan L., 'Not Like Us? Europeans and the Spread of American Culture', *International Affairs*, vol. 74, no. 4, London, October 1998.
Dahrendorf, Ralph, 'The Third Way and Liberty: An Authoritarian Streak in Europe's New Centre', *Foreign Affairs*, vol. 78, No. 5, New York, September/October 1999.
Dilks, David, 'Britain and Europe 1948–1950: The Prime Minister, the Foreign Secretary and the Cabinet', Poidevin, Raymond (ed.), *Histoire des débuts de la Construction Européenne, mars 1948-mai 1950*, Brussels, Milan, Paris, Baden-Baden, 1988.
Dunn, David Hastings, 'Myths, Motivations and "misunderestimations"', *International Affairs*, vol. 79, no. 2, March 2003.
Dunne, Michael, 'The United States, the United Nations and Iraq', *International Affairs*, vol. 79, No. 2, March 2003.
Epstein, Rachel A., Vennesson, Pascal (eds.), *Globalization and Transatlantic Security*, Robert Schuman Centre for Advanced Studies, European University Institute, Florence, Italy, July 2006.

Fellows, Grant Scott, *The Foundation of Alexandr Dugin's Geopolitics*, 1 January 2018, University of Denver, *MA thesis presentation*.
Friedman, Uri, 'Fighting Terrorism with a Credit Card: Interest Payments on America's War Debt Could One Day Exceed the Direct Costs of Combat Itself', *The Atlantic*, 12 September 2016.
Hellman, Gunther (ed.), 'Are Dialogue and Synthesis Possible in International Relations?', *International Studies Review*, Blackwell, Malden (USA), and Oxford, 2003.
Hitchens, Christopher, 'The Perils of Partition', *The Atlantic*, Boston, March 2003.
Holley, Peter, 'Elon Musk's Nightmarish Warning: "AI Could Become "an immortal dictator from which we would never escape"', *Washington Post*, 6 April 2018.
Hough, Andrew, 'Foreign Office Second Language Is Gibberish, Says Plain English Campaign', *Daily Telegraph*, 10 December 2010.
Kasli, Shelley, 'Great Game and Partitioning of Syria', *Oriental Review.com*, 19 March 2016.
Kemp, Geoffrey and Harkavy, Robert E., *Strategic Geography and the Changing Middle East*, Carnegie Endowment for International Peace, Brookings Institute Press, Washington, DC.
Lebow, Richard Ned, 'Fear, Interest and Honour: Outlines of a Theory of International Relations', in op. cit., *International Affairs*, vol. 82.
Mackinder, Halford, 'The Geographical Pivot of History', *Geographical Journal*, vol. 23, no. 4, London, April 1904.
Malashenko, Igor, 'Russia: the Earth's Heartland', *International Affairs*, Moscow, no. 7, July 1990.
Mallinson, William, 'Greece and Cyprus as Geopolitical Fodder, and the Russian Connexion', *Journal of Balkan and Near Eastern Studies*, vol. 22, no. 3, April 2020.
Mallinson, William, 'Turkish Invasions, Britain, Cyprus and the Treaty of Guarantee', *Synthesis, Review of Modern Greek Studies*, vol. 3, no. 1, 1999.
McDonagh, Melanie, 'Sir Humphrey's New Suit', *The Spectator*, 22 January 2011.
Mearsheimer, John and Walt, Stephen, 'The Israel Lobby', *London Review of Books*, 23 March 2006.
Medvedev, Dmitry, 'America 2.0. After the Election', *TASS*, 16 January 2021.
Orwell, George, 'Politics and the English Language', *Horizon*, London, 1946.
Perle, Richard, 'Iraq: Saddam Unbound', in Kagan, Robert and Kristol, William, *Present dangers*, Encounter Books, San Francisco, 2000.
Pilger, John, 'The Most Lethal Virus Is Not Covid. It Is War', *MPN NEWS*, 14 December 2020.

Pocock, J.G.A. (Johns Hopkins University), 'Machiavelli and Guicciardini: Ancients and Moderns', *Canadian Journal of Political and Social Theory/Revue Canadienne de théorie politique et sociale*, vol. 2, no. 3 (Fall/Automne) 1978.
Rengger, Nicholas, 'Political Theory and International Relations: Promised Land or Exit from Eden?', *International Affairs*, vol. 76, no. 4, Blackwell, Oxford, October 2000.
Sked, Alan, 'The Study of International Relations: A Historian's View', Dyer, Hugh C. and Mangasarian, Leon (eds.), *The Study of International Relations*, Macmillan, Basingstoke and London, 1989.
Solovyev, Eduard G., 'Geopolitics in Russia – Science or Vocation?', *Communist and Post-Communist Studies*, vol. 37, no. 1, 1 March 2004.
Strange, Susan, 'States, Firms and Diplomacy', *International Affairs*, vol. 68, no. 1, January 1992, Royal Institute of International Affairs.
Wallace, Paul W. and Orphanides, Andreas G. (eds.), *Sources for the History of Cyprus*, vol. XI, Enosis and the British: British Official Documents 1878–1950, selected and edited by Coughlan, Reed, Greece and Cyprus Research Center, Altamont (Albany, NY, 1990–2004).
Walt, Stephen, 'International Relations: One World, Many Theories', *Foreign Policy*, Washington, Spring 1998.
White, Michael, 'Dalyell Renews Attack on Levy', The Guardian, 6 May 2003
Le Carré, John, Absolute Friends, Coronet Books (Hodder and Stoughton), London, 2004, pp. 267–8.

Index

A
Albania, 91
Albright, Madeleine, 49
Amazon, 108
Ambition, 4, 19, 20, 54, 73, 113, 128, 134, 136
America, 6, 23, 27, 36, 46, 48, 49, 51, 52, 54, 57, 89
Anger, 70, 76, 134, 136
Aristotle, 25, 26
Assad, 56, 79
Atavism, 73, 79, 89, 90, 93, 126–130, 132
Athens, 40, 41, 59, 61–63, 72, 109, 116, 117, 123, 126, 133
Austro-Hungary, 23, 90
Avarice, 19

B
Balance of power, vi, 2, 47, 51–53, 55, 120, 139
Balkans, 22, 23, 57, 79
Barzini, Luigi, 20, 26, 27
Behaviour, v, vi, 2, 3, 10, 17–20, 24, 25, 32, 35, 39, 44, 45, 49, 53, 59, 79, 87, 88, 91, 92, 94, 95, 121, 124, 129, 131, 132, 134, 136
Behaviouralism, 8, 34, 35, 38
Behaviourist, 87
Bismarckian, 35, 123
Blair, 76, 81, 100, 135
Bolsheviks, 6, 59
Bosnia-Herzegovina, 128
Bosniaks, 89
Brexit, 6, 115, 131
British Petroleum (BP), 74, 79
Brzezinski, Zbigniew, 51, 64
Bush Junior, 49, 75
Byron, Lord, 22

C
Callaghan, James, 125, 126
Canning, 22, 134

© The Editor(s) (if applicable) and The Author(s), under exclusive license to Springer Nature Switzerland AG 2021
W. Mallinson, *Guicciardini, Geopolitics and Geohistory*, Palgrave Studies in International Relations,
https://doi.org/10.1007/978-3-030-76537-8

Capitalism, 36, 108
Capodistrias, 21, 57, 60
Categorisation, 8, 36, 115, 131
Characteristics, 2, 10, 17, 24, 25, 39, 44–46, 49, 61, 79, 87, 88, 90–95, 106, 121, 124, 128, 129, 131, 132, 134, 136
Cheney, Dick, 78
Cheney, Richard, 49
Christian Zionism, 128
Christie, Agatha, 44, 62
Churchill, 23, 28, 49, 57, 63
Clinton, 100
Communism, 22, 38, 58
Conceptual framework, 2, 6, 86, 120
Confucius, 101
Constructivism, 8, 27, 36, 38
Counsels and Reflections, 2, 10, 26, 62, 81, 96, 117, 139
Critical theory, 36, 38
Cyprus, 23, 24, 57–62, 67–74, 77, 80, 81, 122, 123, 125, 126

D
Dahrendorf, Ralph, 100, 116
Danilevsky, Nikolai, 53
Dependency theory, 8, 35
Digitalisation, 106, 107, 109, 110, 130, 135
Dilke, Charles, 48, 49
Don Pacifico, 22
Dresden, 133
Dugin, Alexandr, 53, 54, 64

E
England, 3, 24, 49, 69, 93, 127–129, 132, 133
European Union (EU), 53, 56, 60, 68, 72, 73, 76, 131

F
Florence, v, 4, 9, 16, 17, 20, 35, 82, 93, 114
Foreign and Commonwealth Office (FCO), 22, 23, 28, 40, 58, 64, 77, 104, 105, 109, 112–114, 117, 123–125, 138, 139
Foreign, Commonwealth and Development Office (FCDO), 111
Foreign Office (FO), 23, 57, 70, 71, 80, 104, 116, 124, 129
Fukuyama, 7, 38, 41
Functionalism, 8, 36

G
Game theory, 8
Gazprom, 56
Geography, 10, 44–47, 50, 61, 62, 86, 94
Germany, 23, 48–50, 58, 63, 90, 93, 94, 133, 138
Giddens, Anthony, 100, 116
Glaspie, 74
Globalisation, 44, 73, 79, 95, 100–103, 105, 107, 109–112, 115, 116, 120, 130, 135, 136
Google, 108
Great Reset, 107, 108, 110
Greece, 17, 20–23, 36, 37, 46, 52, 57–62, 70, 71, 73, 80, 91
Greed, 4, 19, 79, 88, 89, 91, 107, 110, 120, 133, 134, 136
Grivas, 70, 72, 73
Grotian, 36

H
Halliburton, 78
Haushofer, Karl, 50, 52, 53, 55, 94
Hegel, 45, 50, 95
Hess, Rudolf, 50

Hill, Christopher, 11, 55, 62, 64, 65, 86, 96, 121, 122, 138
Hiroshima, 133
Hitler, 6, 50, 55
Hobbes, Thomas, 3, 6, 19, 32, 35, 36
Huntingdon, Samuel, 7

I

Idealism, 8, 22, 94, 132, 133, 136
Identity, 44, 86, 90, 91, 94, 115, 122, 126, 129–132, 136
Ideology, vi, 2, 7, 8, 15, 36, 39, 46, 50, 56, 86, 87
Imperialism, 46, 62
Imperialistic, 49
Industrial Revolution, 37, 47, 105
Information Commissioner, 123, 138
Interests, v, vi, 2, 5, 6, 18, 20–23, 28, 34, 39, 45, 46, 48, 49, 52, 54, 56, 58–60, 62, 64, 71, 73–75, 77, 86, 89, 92, 108, 109, 114, 120, 122–124, 126–129, 131–134, 136, 137
Internet, 10, 100, 107
Iraq, 27, 35, 56, 61, 62, 67, 68, 70, 73–79, 116, 123, 135
Italy, 3, 5, 6, 9, 16, 17, 35, 48, 52, 61, 82, 90, 93, 127, 129, 132

J

Jealousy, 134, 136
Jewish State, 127

K

Kantian, 36
Katyn, 125
Kennedy, John F., 56, 79
Kissinger, Henry, 3, 11, 34, 51, 52, 64, 72, 77, 124–126, 132, 138, 139

Kjellen, Rudolf, 47, 50
Kurdish, 77

L

Laden, Osama bin, 6
Le Carré, John, 76, 81
Leviathan, 3
Liberalism, vi, 36, 38, 53
Libya, 56, 77
Lyons, Edmund, 22, 57

M

Macedonia, 91, 128, 130
Machiavelli, Niccolò, v, 3–6, 11, 16, 17, 19, 20, 27, 35, 93
Mackinder, Halford, 47–51, 53–55, 63
Mahan, Alfred, 47, 51, 55, 63, 64
Marx, 6, 50, 95
Memory, 2, 86, 87, 111, 112, 116, 120–122, 127
Mensheviks, 6
Meta-imperialism, 46
Metternich, 21, 53, 124, 134
MI6, 135
Ministry of Defence's (MOD), 70, 80
Modernisation theory, 8, 35
Moscow, 58–60, 64, 139, 140
Moslem, 54, 72, 79, 128
Musk, Elon, 106, 117

N

Nagasaki, 133
Nationalism, 48, 115, 128–132, 136
Nation-state, vi, 115, 127, 128, 136
NATO, 23, 24, 54, 57, 58, 60, 61, 68, 89, 90
Nazism, 107
Neocons, 35
Neoliberalism, 38

Neo-Ottomanism, 24, 129, 130
Neorealism, 34, 35, 38
Nikoloyevitch, 53
Normative theory, 8, 32, 36

O

Oil, 10, 54, 56, 58, 61, 74, 75, 77–79, 89, 115
Orwell, George, 62, 102
Oscar Wilde, 9, 138
Ottoman, 20–22, 57, 60, 68–70, 74, 90, 91, 129, 132, 133
Ó Tuathail, Gearóid, 55, 63, 64

P

Palmerston, 132, 134, 139
Paradigm, vi, 26, 38, 39, 86, 137
Pitt, William, 20, 47, 57
Pluralism, 8, 36–38
Poland, 6
Positivism, 8, 35
Post-modernism, 36, 38
Power, 3–6, 10, 16, 17, 19, 21, 23, 25, 34–37, 45–48, 50–53, 55, 62, 65, 67–69, 74, 75, 77, 86, 90, 105–109, 121, 129, 133–135
Power politics, 3, 6, 10, 25, 34, 35, 41, 51, 62, 68
Prejudice, 121, 136
Pride, 90, 91, 134, 136

Q

Qatar, 56
Qatari, 56, 79

R

Raison d'état, 5, 6, 126, 129, 136
Rambouillet, 90
Ranke, 6

Ratzel, Friedrich, 47, 48, 50
Realism, vi, 3, 19, 25, 32, 34, 36, 38, 39, 41, 45, 62, 86, 88, 122
Realpolitik, 7, 34, 35, 38, 41, 60, 123
Rice, Condoleezza, 49
Rumsfeld, Donald, 49
Russia, 20–24, 45, 47, 48, 50, 51, 53, 54, 56–61, 68–70, 73, 77, 89, 90, 102

S

Saddam Hussein, 74, 79
Schwab, Klaus, 108, 110
Serbia, 54, 89, 90, 109, 138
Sèvres, 130
Slavs, 89, 91, 96
Somerset Maugham, William, 102, 139
Sovereign Base Areas (SBAs), 60, 71, 80
Soviet Union, 22, 23, 53, 56, 57, 59, 63, 68, 77, 133
Sparta, 3, 4
Speed, 79, 105, 107, 110, 111, 116, 120, 135, 136
Spykman, Nicholas John, 51, 63
Stalin, 23, 57, 59
State, vi, 2, 4, 6–8, 10, 16, 17, 19–21, 32, 34–40, 44, 47, 50, 52–59, 61, 62, 65, 68, 71–75, 77, 85, 86, 88–94, 96, 101, 102, 109, 110, 115, 116, 120, 122–124, 126–136
Strauss, Leo, 3, 11, 35, 41
Structuralism, 8, 35, 38
Sykes-Picot, 54, 56, 74, 76, 89
Syria, 56, 68, 79, 89, 90

T

Taylor, A.J.P., 53, 64, 138
The Prince, 3, 11, 27

Third Way, 100
Thucydides, 3, 4, 6, 11, 17, 19, 20, 27, 35, 61, 65
Tolstoy, Leo, 135, 140
Trilateral Commission, 109
Truman Doctrine, 23, 57, 59
Turkey, 20, 21, 23, 24, 56, 58–61, 68–73, 90, 91, 126, 129, 130, 139
Twitter, 103, 104, 113, 114, 135

U
United Nations (UN), 71, 72, 74, 81, 133
United States (US), 6, 23, 27, 45, 46, 48, 51, 52, 55–61, 63, 72–79, 90, 106, 109, 123, 127, 132, 133, 135

V
Vanity, 136

Versailles, 132
Vico, Giambattista, 49, 87, 96, 120, 138

W
Washington, 41, 60, 63, 75, 81, 124
Wellington, 21
Wight, Martin, 11, 26, 27, 52, 64
Wolfowitz, Paul, 35, 49, 76, 81
World systems analysis, 8, 35

Y
Yalta, 23
Younghusband, 48
Yugoslavia, 22, 23, 57, 128, 129
Yutang, Lin, 37, 40

Z
Zionist, 75, 76

Printed in the United States
by Baker & Taylor Publisher Services